School Isn't For Everyone
(and what you can do instead)

of related interest

A Different Way to Learn
Neurodiversity and Self-Directed Education
Naomi Fisher
Illustrated by Eliza Fricker
ISBN 978 1 83997 363 5
eISBN 978 1 83997 950 7

Can't Not Won't
A Story About A Child Who Couldn't Go To School
Eliza Fricker
ISBN 978 1 83997 520 2
eISBN 978 1 80501 696 0

The Parent's Handbook to Unschooling Yourself
A Mindful Guide to Embracing a New Way of Living and Learning With Your Child
Esther Jones
ISBN 978 1 80501 275 7
eISBN 978 1 80501 276 4

SCHOOL isn't for EVERYONE (and what you can do instead)

A practical neuro-affirming guide to unschooling

Heidi Steel

Foreword by Naomi Fisher

Illustrated by Becky Whinnerah

Jessica Kingsley Publishers
London and Philadelphia

First published in Great Britain in 2026 by Jessica Kingsley Publishers
An imprint of John Murray Press

2

A CIP catalogue record for this title is available from the British Library and the Library of Congress

ISBN 978 1 80501 805 6
eISBN 978 1 80501 806 3

Printed and bound in the United States by Integrated Books International

Jessica Kingsley Publishers' policy is to use papers that are natural, renewable and recyclable products and made from wood grown in sustainable forests. The logging and manufacturing processes are expected to conform to the environmental regulations of the country of origin.

Jessica Kingsley Publishers
Carmelite House
50 Victoria Embankment
London EC4Y 0DZ

www.jkp.com

John Murray Press
Part of Hodder & Stoughton Ltd
An Hachette Company

The authorised representative in the EEA is Hachette Ireland, 8 Castlecourt Centre, Dublin 15, D15 XTP3, Ireland (email: info@hbgi.ie)

For my children, who took what I knew and turned it into something extraordinary.

Contents

Foreword

I first met Heidi Steel when our oldest children were aged eight and seven. Neither of us had much time to think, and even less time to chat. Our eyes met as we rushed past each other, juggling the various needs of our children. We were both pulled in many directions. But we had one thing firmly in common – we were both unschooling, home educating our children without a formal curriculum.

It felt like a counter-cultural thing to do. Other children were going to school. They were learning how to read and write, how to sit on their bottoms and put their hand up before speaking. Ours weren't, and it really showed. At that point none of them were reading or writing and there was very little sitting still. They spent all their time playing, and the oldest children were getting beyond the point where the rest of the world thought that was okay. We were facing questions like 'What about GCSEs?' and 'You mean you're just leaving reading up to chance?'

Over the years we continued to meet up, and as the children got older there was more time to talk. In snatched moments around Heidi's kitchen table we'd discuss how unschooling was so much more than 'leaving it up to chance' and yet people couldn't see it. We talked about how frustrating it was to be spending so much energy facilitating our children's learning and to have it dismissed as 'So you just do nothing then?' We'd talk about how we struggled to explain unschooling to others who were looking for the workbooks and curriculums we didn't use.

We discussed how most people thought that learning was 'what goes on at school' and were unaware of the amazing process that was unfurling in front of our eyes. How we had both started unschooling with very little idea of what that would look like as our children grew older, and how hard it is to trust the process when the schooled eight-year-olds are doing extensive written projects on Ancient Egypt and your unschooled child spends most of their time hanging upside down and playing *Terraria*.

We'd talk about what we observed. We saw how our children were developing in ways that Heidi, an experienced teacher, and I, a clinical psychologist, hadn't been taught about in our training. We saw them learning things without formal instruction that we had thought must be taught at school.

We didn't know what the future would bring for them. We didn't really know any unschooled teenagers, and we worried about things like 'What if they never want to learn how to write by hand?' and 'How will they ever learn to stick at things?' We were both driven by a strong sense that even though we couldn't know what the future would bring, we were doing the best we could for our children right now. We were meeting their needs as the children they were, rather than anticipating and fearing the future.

That meant play, in many different forms. Heidi is exceptionally good at creating a stimulating play environment. One particularly memorable day we had planned a spot of light finger painting, but the children took it far beyond our intentions. Before we knew it, the three youngest children were stripping off and 'ice skating' in paint next to the washing machine. That adventure ended in the bath, where the murky water provided more opportunities for play.

When I look back over those years, the paint skating day represents so many other experiences. Heidi and I had some ideas and provided the resources, but the children consistently had more exciting ideas that they pursued in a single-minded fashion. Our role was often to try to mitigate the chaos created in their wake. Slime explosions, cakes without recipes – almost everything went a step or two further than we had anticipated. The conventional choice would have been to say 'no', to keep them on track and to restrict the activity to what we had planned. Finger painting, not full body painting. Drawing on the paper, not on the walls.

Following the recipes, not adding in anything we can find in the cupboard.

Whenever possible, we made a different choice. We went with the flow and dealt with the mess afterwards. I started to see how those moments were when unschooling really took off. The children took what was available and discovered something new. They experimented, and as they did so, they learned.

Years have passed and our children are now teenagers. They no longer skate in paint. My children have attended democratic schools and learning communities, while Heidi has continued to unschool. I now know from my own experience that children can learn to read without a formal curriculum, and that teenagers can set themselves goals for the future without being compelled to do so. I know that much of what happens at school is not necessary for learning. I've seen young people choosing to learn a whole range of subjects, including things that are challenging and that require long periods of sustained effort. I've seen teenagers who haven't gone to school taking exams and excelling at college. As I've met more self-directed teenagers, I've been blown away by how much they see themselves as the active agent in their own learning. If they want to learn something, they do not wait to be taught; they go out there and find a way for themselves.

It is in those teenagers that we can see what unschooling is all about. For unschooling has at its heart the idea that children do not need to be compelled to learn, and that by compelling them we can do lasting damage. In young children, this means years and years of play. It means spending their time doing things adults frequently do not value. Video games, Barbies and collecting Pokémon, for example. It's hard to see the progress in those early years, and easy to compare them with schooled children and panic. It can be hard to see the way ahead.

That's where this wonderful book comes in. Heidi has an unparalleled depth of experience. She has not only unschooled her own four children for 18 years (so far), runs courses as an unschooling coach and administers local unschooling groups, but has also worked for over a decade as a teacher. There isn't much about learning outside school that Heidi hasn't thought about. She knows the highs and the lows inside out.

In this book, she shares that experience with you, describing what to expect as your children grow up and as you settle into unschooling. She draws on interviews with other unschooling parents to illustrate what the different phases of unschooling look like. She knows what the frequent 'wobble points' are, and she answers the questions you might have bouncing around in your head. It's unlikely that you've got a query that Heidi hasn't been asked before.

This makes this book an essential guide to all those unschooling parents wondering, *is it meant to look like this?* It's the place to turn when all the children around you are starting school and you're wondering if it really is okay to just carry on as you did before. It's the thing to read when you're wondering what your children actually are learning, since they don't want to do anything you suggest. It's the book to open when it's clear that school isn't working for your child, but you're not sure what you could do instead.

It will help you to see your child's learning, even when it looks like nothing.

Heidi and I first talked about writing books several years ago in one of those snatched moments at her kitchen table. Now we are at the point where we have both achieved that dream. I was delighted to be asked to write a foreword to this book, which feels in many ways like a full circle. I hope that it will give many other unschooling families the inspiration that Heidi and I found in each other.

I hope it will give you the confidence to help your child to learn in ways that don't look anything like school.

Naomi Fisher, clinical psychologist, author and speaker specialising in autism, trauma, parenting and alternative education

Acknowledgements

I sat in a room, chairs and tables stacked around the edges, with a handful of local unschooling families. My younger two crawled under the stacked tables with a few other young children. My older two had decided not to come. I went anyway, it sounded interesting, and I wondered if I could take some of the ideas back home with me. Parents and teens sat on chairs facing the front. There stood an adult, alongside their PowerPoint presentation and whiteboard, and they asked the question, 'What is it that you want to do?' And I knew, in that moment, that I wanted to write a book about unschooling.

That was at the beginning of 2020, and thanks to many a person since then it has been made possible. I still can't quite get over the fact that I get to use the phrase 'my editor', but Lynda's gentle hand holding has been invaluable along the way and meant that I have managed to keep my stress levels fairly low. To the lovely Rachel who has listened to me from the beginning, questioning whether this was even possible to musing over ideas, I am thankful for your time and wisdom. Thanks to Naomi who has cheered me on from the start and had unwavering faith in me. To Jenny, who has listened to me, encouraged me and has loved me through many seasons. I wouldn't be where I am today without you. And to those in our local home ed community, all of whom have listened to me talk more about this book than they probably would have liked but, more importantly, have made our unschooling journey possible. They have walked alongside me and my family through the ups and downs of life, not just the creation of this book, and I am thankful for every one of you and all your glorious young people.

This book wouldn't have been possible without the wonderful contributions from Chloe, Jess, Alice, Nicola, Nici, Sally, Sorrel, Rebecca, Susan, May Ling, Steve and Sarah. I had such an amazing time chatting with you all. It was so hard choosing what stories and words to share as you all gave so beautifully. I don't think I encapsulated your passion for unschooling in all the vibrancy with which you shared it, but I am so grateful that you entrusted your words to me, and I know that they will make a difference to those who read them.

And finally, to my family, my children, who led me to explore the depths of unschooling and reveal now, even after all these years, how schooled my thinking is. And my husband Matthew, who tried to hide his shock when I first mentioned that I thought four children would be a good idea but didn't bat an eyelid when I suggested that we home educate them. It is not a straightforward life and it is not an easy option, but watching our children flourish and thrive in their own unique ways is both a privilege and a delight.

Introduction

I lead a pretty regular life. I get up in the morning, normally eat the same thing for breakfast every day, shower and dress, and then spend some time catching up on emails and doing work-related admin. I'll check my diary for the day and work out what I need to put in my bag to take out with me, what time I need to leave, and think about what there is in the house for dinner. I have lists of things to do everywhere, which I will either approach with ferocity and complete in a matter of a morning or I will avoid for weeks on end. I enjoy my garden, I attempt gardening, I love watching and listening to the birds, I spend my time reading, binge-watching TV series, watching films, knitting and crochet, and when I get a chance (we'll come back to that later) I like cooking new recipes. I also have two cats, a dog, four chickens, four pet rats and one fish. All typical stuff.

As I write this, I am painfully aware that it hasn't always been this way and isn't as straightforward as it sounds. I have reached a point in my life where my children are all over the age of seven. I have four children (which is a little unusual) and none of them have ever been to school. That tends to be the point when others consider my life to be different. It also tends to be the point where the topic of conversation takes a turn and focuses solely on home educating: 'What do you do all day?' 'How do you teach your own children?' 'How can you spend all your time with them?' 'Do they have any friends?' 'What if they want to become a brain surgeon?' 'How do you find any time for yourself?' 'Who inspects you?' 'Do you use a curriculum?' 'How do you know if they are doing enough?' 'Is that legal?' 'What about exams and qualifications?'

It turns out that choosing a life that is totally different to what people know conjures up all kinds of responses. We are mostly met by others with curiosity and genuine intrigue. We exchange pleasantries and I briefly answer their questions (or I nod and smile while they chatter on, because sometimes people don't want to hear the answers – they just want to share their own school stories and parenting choices with you). The truth is, though, that they don't know the half of it. I tend to stick to the basics. 'Yes, you are legally allowed to home educate in the UK', 'Home-educated children can take exams if and when they want to', 'My children have lots of friends, we know a lot of other home-educating families.' Probably as close as I get to stretching the thinking of someone new to the idea is, 'We spend our days learning about the things that we choose to' or 'We don't use a curriculum; they choose what they learn'.

I became fascinated with how children learn when I did my work experience in my local primary school when I was in Year 11 (aged 16). I remember sitting with a young child, maybe five or six years old, trying to solve a maths question. This child did not understand the question and did not know how to work out the answer. I sat with them and drew pictures and got cubes to help them figure it out. And they did. I don't remember the question, I don't remember the explanation, I don't remember how they got to the answer, but I do remember their face when they had figured it out, and I remember the feeling that it gave me when they had grasped it. I thought at that point that my interest was in teaching, and that experience set me on a pathway to becoming a qualified primary school teacher.

During my training, I specialised in Early Years and became immersed in studying child development and was introduced to neuroscience and cognitive development. I absolutely loved it. I spent hours and hours observing young children at play, and was guided in my first few teaching years by others who drew my attention to the amazing things that children do and learn all by themselves. Early Years settings were absolutely my favourite place to be. I spent 14 years working in primary schools and had a whole range of experiences working under different headships and in different counties, even in different countries. By the time I came to have my own children, and they legally reached 'compulsory school age', I knew that children were fully capable and able to learn, develop and grow without the intervention of school or a curriculum, and armed with this knowledge, I decided to home educate my children. Not only that, I decided that I was going to do it according to their own natural pathways, and I was going to support them in their own developmental trajectory because I knew that they were capable of learning what they needed to, when they needed to learn it.

And so, it turns out, my life is not so regular after all. I spend my days alongside my children. I help them to do the things that they choose to do. I take them to places that interest them. I watch the shows that they want to watch. I clear up the mess that they make after they have made a magical potion or the 'Best Cake Ever', I watch the show that they have made on the trampoline, I play *Minecraft* and make stop motion films with LEGO® or Barbies. We meet with other families who also live this life, we play in the local parks, go to the beach, climb trees in the woods, visit museums, take classes together, and have play dates in each other's homes.

For the past 16 years I have facilitated the education and life choices of my four children on a daily basis. We have surrounded ourselves with friends and built a community that shares our outlook and values. This has become our norm. This has become my every day. And so, for me, it feels like a regular life.

This book explores how to move towards unschooling. There is no one set path or step-by-step programme, but there is a common trajectory. This book address questions that families often ask me, and frequent barriers that arise as families begin to consider alternatives to traditional schooling. It shows what is possible when you leave school behind and start living a life of learning. I have drawn on current theory and evidence while sharing practical tips and being grounded in the reality of day-to-day life with children. The book does this by including interviews with unschooling families, exercises for you to help consider ideas, providing diagrams to illustrate the concepts being explored and listing key principles at the end of every chapter. Notably each chapter will be introduced with a black and white illustration encapsulating the key thought being explored, drawn by Becky Whinnerah.

As the book moves along the trajectory from school to unschool the chapters include thoughts on how school shapes our views about education and learning; how neurodivergent children are the canaries in the mine; what unschooling is and is not; the process of adjustment; the importance of play in childhood; what natural learning looks like; the difference that unschooling makes to your child's life experience; and what you can do to support your child and their learning. It also answers common questions on socialising, learning to read, the teenage years and screen time, and provides you with the key ingredient to unleashing a life of learning.

What I desire for you is to become so confident and comfortable with a different kind of education that it comes with ease even though you are doing something so extraordinarily different.

Chapter 1

When School Is a Problem

Reading the Signs and Finding a Way Forward

I don't believe that school is fit for purpose. I'm pretty sure that you have similar misgivings because you are holding this book in your hands. You are here looking for something different, and it can be an uneasy place to be. On the one hand is a school system that thinks it's the bee's knees and everyone in it is telling you that it is the best (and only) place for your child to get an education. On the other hand there are signs, some small, others big and glaring, and some you feel unsure about and can't quite put your finger on, but nonetheless you are feeling that maybe school is not the best place for your child.

Most of us have been to school (currently only 1.4 per cent of children in England are home educated[1]). Most parents automatically send their children to school in the UK at the age of four, unaware that 'compulsory school age' isn't until the term after their fifth birthday. Legal requirements around the world vary, but most families follow the norm unquestioningly. Even if you were aware, requesting a flexible approach is rarely granted, and waiting until your child turns five limits your options because there are then fewer spaces available as most parents register their children at an earlier entry point. Even the term 'compulsory school age' gives the impression that school is compulsory. *Education is compulsory, school is not.*

School is part of our cultural make-up. It is so prevalent that most people don't question its existence. It governs our days and our family life, and for the most part it is our only experience of education. We have heard the messages on repeat about the need to pay attention, get top marks and pass exams. We have been told that this is how we will be successful in life and that missing any school will have catastrophic effects on our future. (Anyone else remember being told that they will end up living under a bridge if they didn't make it to class?)

School has shaped our views about how children should be taught, what teaching looks like and how learning happens. School was built and designed for a reason, and there have always been signs that school isn't for everyone. Children up and down the country are telling us that school is stressful, and irrelevant, and parents are questioning behavioural policies and the developmental appropriateness of some schools' requirements. It doesn't change the fact

1 Department for Education (2024) 'Elective home education. Autumn term 2024/25.' https://explore-education-statistics.service.gov.uk/find-statistics/elective-home-education

that choosing to do something different, to take full responsibility for your child's education, is a big decision.

As a teacher I witnessed firsthand how the system works. My specialty was Early Years, and I am sure if I had worked continuously in any other year group I would have left the teaching profession earlier! I spent 14 years working in primary schools, mostly in Reception classes where children largely spend their days in play and play-based activities. This is where my interest in how children truly learn began. I was fortunate to find myself in places that heralded learning through play, invested heavily in creating rich spaces for children to play in and committed to training of staff. This is where I saw for myself that all children are fully equipped and able to learn naturally, which was in stark contrast to my work in primary school Years 1–6, where classrooms told a very different story. From within the classroom walls I got to see how the change from child-centred to teacher-led approaches happened and the impact this had on children, and began to question why it was necessary.

A brief history of school (as we know it)

The education system as we know it is the result of hundreds of years of evolution. It is derived from influences from politics, religion and economics, and has been impacted by countries developing educational practices worldwide. In the context of exploring it in juxtaposition to unschooling, the aspects that are of interest to us are: when, how and why did play become unimportant in society? And when did we stop trusting children to learn, develop and grow in accordance with their own natural ability to do so?

Let's start with the shift away from children and adults living playful lives in community with each other. Once upon a time people lived in a culture of curiosity, playfulness, trust, respect and care. Hunter-gather people groups had swathes of free time and pursuits that were needed for survival, were highly skilled, and required a deep knowledge of plants, the terrain and weather systems, among other things, which were all passed on and learned through skills sharing and experience.[1] It was the dawn of agriculture that brought around a change in attitude towards children, play and work. With cultivated land came increasing amounts of required work for successful crop production. It was all hands to the plough and less time to play.

Agricultural society also brought with it ownership of land and the building of property. In short, it was the beginnings of wealth and status. Society was slowly becoming hierarchical, with those who owned more wealth and property exerting power over those with less. This included the ownership of people, slavery and child labour, and an ever-strengthening idea that others could be controlled through force, violence and fear. This system based on hierarchy slowly became reflected within the family too, where men became leaders in their own homes, women were to serve their husbands, and children were to be moulded into obedient and useful members of the household and society.

Before schools, as we know them, were even a concept, children were considered as chattels and in need of moulding to a desired outcome. Play in society had been largely removed from daily life and vilified, even in childhood. It was seen as an unworthy pursuit and signified frivolity, laziness and loss of self-control, all of which were considered abhorrent and sinful. Toil was established as a worthy pursuit, and systems based on hierarchy within the workplace, religious settings and the family grew to be the norm.

Schools did exist, though, in some form. In their earliest iterations, we can see traits that were established and have remained over the years and developed into what is now commonplace. There were schools for the elite (mostly males) to learn Latin so that they could enter the priesthood, and there were private tutors for those who could afford them. Then came grammar schools and universities, again, for the upper classes. Alongside this came the rise of church schools that specifically taught literacy to the masses. There were also apprenticeship programmes for skilled labour.

1 Gray, Peter (2015) *Free to Learn: Why Unleashing the Instinct to Play Will Make Our Children Happier, More Self-Reliant, and Better Students for Life*. Basic Books.

Keep in mind that these places were not mandatory in any way. The ages of the children that they catered for varied significantly, the number of days and weeks that they were open were few, and for the most part children were working on their family farms or businesses. There was a general apathy towards attending school and learning, as parents saw it as a way of separating children from their family and depriving them of working hands. Force, violence and fear were standard within schools as they became tools used for compliance. This approach established teachers and head teachers in service to the government and children being required to conform. The hierarchy established in those first schools remains firmly in place today and has a significant effect on how our children, and we, learn in mainstream schools.

The tale of two schools (of thought)

It wasn't until the late 1800s that we see the first school established by a governing body that was free for everybody. The Prussian education system was the first of its kind introducing compulsory education for 5- to 13-year-olds, requiring certified teachers, separating pupils by age, and overseen nationally.[2] The system was developed specifically to indoctrinate children into compliance with the state and specifically, at the time, the military. American and British schools to this day are largely based on this model whereby children are taught by qualified professionals only, classes are separated by age, and it is all overseen by the government, which controls content through curriculum.

In the UK, it was the Industrial Revolution that changed the landscape of education and ushered in compulsory (but not free) education for 5- to 10-year-olds in 1876. It is unsurprising that schools mirrored factory-like conditions and systems. The primary goal was to prepare children for factory work by instilling discipline, obedience and basic literacy skills. As a result, schools adopted standardised curriculums and fixed schedules, and required

2 Imix, Jyoti (2022) *What to Do About School* [Self-published].

conformity. The bell system, still used in schools today, further echoed the factory-like conditions and prepared children for their future working life.

In 1891 primary education became free in the UK.[1] Learning became the work of childhood. Learning skills that they could go on to use in the factories became the goal. Learning in systems that instructed them in the ways of employment became the method.

Free secondary education raised the school leaving age from 14 to 15 in 1947. To put this into context, this means that many of our parents and grandparents were the first to have free access to secondary education, and higher education continued to be accessible only to those who could finance it themselves or acquire a scholarship.

It wasn't necessarily that culturally we stopped trusting children to learn; more that it had become alien in society, and that those in power purposefully created an education system that replicated the factory set-up and resulted in skilled workers. School was never designed for children; it was designed by and for those in power to produce an obedient and skilled workforce.[2]

Not that far away, on the European continent, a man named Friedrich Froebel was forming his ideas on the role of children's play in human development. He came to believe that play was the principle means of learning in early childhood, and in 1836 he established the first 'kindergarten' for children under the age of seven.[3] It was a dramatically different approach to setting up organised spaces for children and its influence can be seen within some mainstream schools today, but is more common in alternative education settings. You will mostly be familiar with play-based learning in quality preschools and Reception classes. Children have access to resources, spaces and adults they can use to play with, all day, in ways that suit them.

From the dawn of formal education there has continued to be this collision between these two approaches. On the one hand, an

1 See www.education-uk.org/history/timeline.html

2 Barber, Jean (1997) *A Backward Glance*. Ilkeston and District Local History Society.

3 www.froebel.org.uk/about-us/the-power-of-play

educational pedagogy that prioritises outcomes set by the governing body of the time, and on the other, an educational pedagogy that supports and facilitates a child's growth and development through their natural and innate ability to learn through play and exploration. Most educational methods and philosophies can be traced back to these two practices.

But let us not forget that while government has increased its educational provision, it has always been the parents' responsibility to see that 'every child of compulsory school age shall cause him [sic] to receive efficient full time education suitable to: the child's age, ability, and aptitude, and any special educational needs the child may have, either by regular attendance at school or otherwise'.[4] This includes home education.

The teacher who left teaching

I went straight from completing my A-levels to university and embarked on a four-year teacher training course. I specialised in Early Years education and began my career in a fantastic school that valued the importance of play. Right from those first days I was fascinated with how children learned through their play and had no need for adult-imposed teaching. It's easy to see now why home educating was the inevitable choice for me.

By the time that my eldest child was nearing Reception age (four years old) I had been teaching for over 14 years in over 20 schools and had taught over 1000 children. There were many contributing factors that led us to home educate and specifically unschool our children. My knowledge and understanding of how children learned and learned well through play was one of them. During my time in teaching primary age children, I also questioned a great many other things. Here are a few of the things I witnessed:

- *Children being penalised, pressured, shamed or judged for not being at the same standard as their peers, or singled out and*

4 Section 7, Education Act 1996: www.legislation.gov.uk/ukpga/1996/56/contents

elevated when they showed an aptitude for a specific subject. I saw, firsthand, the effect that constantly being told you are not good enough had on a child's self-esteem, confidence and worth. Even seemingly small and practical things like separating children into ability groups has consequences on class dynamics, friendships and peer interaction. Conversely, those who were singled out because of their talents were often isolated, and this came with its own pressures to maintain those high standards.

- *The constant focus on targets, achievements and test scores and devising ways to improve teaching that ignored the impact on both teachers and the children.* There was no room for a bad day, upset because a pet had died, turmoil from family break-ups, consideration for children who were also young carers, refugee children or simply falling over in the playground. There was little to no room for anything that distracted from the curriculum or fulfilling the next set of learning intentions. It was impersonal and mechanical.

- *The children who had identified special needs who were separated during class so that they could take extra supported sessions doing things they hated.* These singled the children out within the class and often meant that they were missing activities that they felt relaxed in or were good at. For example, it wasn't uncommon for those diagnosed as dyslexic to endure years of tailored reading programmes and one-to-one lessons during an art or music class, which were things that they enjoyed.

- *The increasing amount of pressure that Reception teachers were under to introduce lessons that replicated the approach taken further up the school.* Enabling play was being pushed to the sidelines and its significance seriously diminished in schools without a strong Early Years lead or head teacher with a good understanding of the essential role of play. There have always been discussions around the idea that in the UK children are required to do 'too much, too soon' when other approaches don't even consider formal teaching until a child is over the age of seven. Now we are witnessing 'even more, even sooner'.

- *The number of children who turn up to school on day one full of fire and excitement and six weeks later they have lost their spark (sometimes as little as the following day!)*. Children were sold the excitement of school and enjoyed it for a while, but the realisation dawned on them that this is it now, that there is no opt out. And then there are those children who make it clear that they don't want to be there in the first place, those who are not ready to be separated from their main caregiver or their family, some of whom eventually comply, but others don't.

- *Little room for individuality*. We see this play out in secondary or high schools with stricter uniform rules (among other things), but it begins in primary and elementary schools. Once a week you might be able to share something at 'Show and tell' (but don't forget that it needs to be socially acceptable or exceptional). When a child asks a question that is related to a topic in school it must be relevant to the curriculum being taught (and that's if they are lucky enough to be able to ask questions at all!). Teachers are wizards at being able to turn an 'off topic' question into one that matches the focus for the day. Children's interests and their own curiosity is slowly replaced with the idea that the teacher knows best and what the curriculum dictates is important.

- *Children literally robbed of the idea that they can learn anything for themselves*. It is universally accepted that children need to be taught in order for them to learn. This is largely true when what they should be learning is already laid out for them and there is no room for diversion; it becomes a self-fulfilling prophecy. It also has the effect of convincing children that they need a teacher and that they are unable to learn things for themselves. Any interests or hobbies that the child has outside of school have less value and worth simply because they aren't measurable or 'on the test'. There is an endless list of possibilities open for exploration that is not only reduced but also vilified in favour of exactly and only what is on the curriculum.

These are a few of the things I witnessed from within the school walls. You will have your own list because there are many indicators that school is not a great place for children (in general) and also a specific list of reasons why school is not suitable for your child. Undeniably my experience in a range of different schools, over a 14-year period, informed my perception about schools and the education system. I knew that school was not the best place for children and that the education system is, in my opinion, broken.

The importance of family

School has a deep impact on our lives, and not just from its structure, format and messaging. It seeps into our daily and family life from beyond its four walls. It dictates what time we get up in the morning and subsequently what time we go to bed. It slices away at our finances with school uniform requirements, trips and termly fairs. It requires an increasing number of hours doing homework. It eats into what might be considered family time together, including when holidays can be taken, which also has financial implications. There is little let-up for us as parents; it impacts our family relationships and places the focus on school for most of our time with our children. Honestly, I am exhausted just writing about it.

For those who are adopting conscious parenting approaches, this impact is palpable and jarring to family dynamics. There is little let-up or space to purely be together or enjoy time that is not encroached on by some school-based need or notion. The system and its all-encompassing presence is at odds with your lifestyle. This, too, can be a sign that school isn't for your child or your family.

Personally, I saw the irony in having taught thousands of children only to hand over my own children for someone else to have that pleasure. I enjoyed being with my own children. It wasn't all unicorns and rainbows, but I wasn't in a hurry to be without them and they weren't in a hurry to be without me. Being together suited us as a family, so it was logical that we would do that for as long as everyone was happy with it. Putting my children in school would have had a negative effect on our family dynamics, impacted the parenting approach and relationships we were building and ignored what was (to me) the obvious place for my children to be. It would have also ignored the fact that each of my children, for their own reasons, were not ready to go to school at the age of four.

When I left teaching specifically to home educate my own children, I did not know anyone else who was home educating, and certainly no one who was unschooling. I was, though, certain and confident in my choice to do so. My academic knowledge and years of experience equipped me for the task ahead; however, it also left me with a lot of unlearning to do. It is important to note, and be clear, that you do not need to be a qualified teacher (or a qualified anything) to be an unschooling parent. While my background had led me to this point, it also brought with it its own challenges. It is common to come to home education full of questions and unknowing. I hope this book will not only answer some of those questions and make your own thinking clearer, but actively encourage you to ask more questions and whole-heartedly embrace not knowing as you explore something new.

There are many reasons that parents choose to home educate their children. They are all valid. Even if you don't have a specific reason and you are merely exercising your legal responsibility to educate your child other than at school, it is a valid choice to make.

There are as many ways to home educate as there are home educators. This is one of the beautiful things about not being in school. You get to choose how your child is receiving a suitable education, and it is so flexible that it can look different on any given day and can be different from one sibling to another. Home educating certainly allows for learning to change as your child does.

What is unschooling?

This book focuses on unschooling. You can find attempts to define unschooling across the internet – well established unschooling names trying their best to succinctly and concisely explain what unschooling is. I am going to add my attempt to the throng, but I can tell you now that it won't do it justice or describe the richness and depth of the life it affords. I often describe home education as opening a door onto a whole new world that you didn't know previously existed, and as if that wasn't enough, unschooling is like finding the wardrobe in that world and discovering Narnia.

Unschooling is a self-directed approach to learning undertaken within the family set-up. It is an evidence-based educational philosophy that rests on the understanding that learning is an innate human characteristic, that **children are natural learners**, and that given the right conditions they can flourish and thrive. It recognises in practice that children do not need school to learn. Neither do they need school at home. No curriculums, no workbooks, no timetables, no set hours, no teacher/adult-imposed learning activities. It is not school in every way possible that I can think of.

It recognises that humans learn best when they are interested and enjoying the things they are doing. This, in turn, requires parents to trust what their child is doing, and more than that, to create a life in which they can do more of those things, in ways that are meaningful to them. As parents we come alongside our child, joining them in exploring their passions and facilitating their natural learning.

It recognises that children are fully equipped to learn but we don't leave them to do so by themselves. Unschooling rests, and thrives, in the relationships in our families and communities. Learning well happens when children are safe and secure in their primary relationships and can explore confidently from that point.

More than that, unschooling becomes a lifestyle. Unschooling is often referred to as 'life learning' because as a family you begin to lean into a life not moulded by school or schooled ideas. It changes the choices you have and enables you to consider possibilities you were previously restricted by.

Phew! There are a lot of big ideas in there and things that need taking a closer look at. It doesn't do unschooling justice to reduce it to a few paragraphs, and it often raises more questions than it answers. Even more frustrating than that is that no one can tell you that you must do this or that for unschooling to happen in your home. What it looks like for you and your family will be different to what it looks like in mine. It is not an imposed curriculum or a set of rules that everyone must fit themselves in to follow; it is a set of guiding principles that empower you to make decisions that enable relationships and learning to thrive in your home.

Principles, not rules

Unschooling is nothing like school. It is a radically different approach to education that not only requires you to remove your child from school but, further to that, to remove school from your life. School is a standardised approach to teaching and is supplemented by many rules about how that happens and what good teaching looks like. Unschooling, on the other hand, is based on principles, not rules. Families apply these principles to their own lives and nurture what unfolds before them.

In this book I am going to begin to explore school practices that form our views on education and unpack some of the reasons why they are used in schools and the effects they are having on our children. It might seem strange to include talk about school in a book about unschooling, but unless you understand where you have come from, it is hard to fully let go and move towards where you are going. Mostly, though, I am going to talk about unschooling and introduce you to some of the principles that shape what life looks like for unschooling families. These are the ideas that guide the decisions we make on a day-to-day basis. They steer the ship! They are the concepts that help shape the foundations of your child's education. These key points are listed at the end of each chapter and set in bold throughout the book. Each chapter includes exercises along the way to give you a moment to take a beat and reflect on your thinking and practices. There are going to be lots of tips for you, practical ideas and stories from my own observations because reality can be very different from the theory.

Throughout this book I am going to introduce you to a host of unschooling families who have graciously given up their time to be interviewed and to share their experiences with you. All of them have left the school system behind and found a new way for their children to live and learn. It is my honour to introduce you to such a wide variety of families who have all taken on the principles of unschooling and seen the delight that it has brought to their children, themselves and their families. Their stories are here to demonstrate how these principles are applied to everyone's unique situations and how unschooling can look in different families.

Is unschooling an option for you?

The truth is that unschooling is full on, and it isn't for the faint-hearted.

Families from all walks of life can and do unschool. Families from all over the world and in all sorts of different situations unschool and unschool well. What unschooling needs more than the perfect set-up, the perfect location, perfect timing or the perfect situation is parents who are willing to unschool.

Unschooling needs parents who are keen to spend time with their children. To be present, available and attentive. Parents who can come alongside and support their child in the things that they find meaningful and in ways that they engage best in. Children need unschooling parents who are resourceful, inquisitive and active participants in their child's life. The unschooling parent is committed to journeying with their child.

Alongside this unschooling parents are often naturally curious themselves. They find life, or specific aspects of life, interesting, and can share their sense of awe and wonder with those around them. They bring a 'can do' attitude to the table, complete with skills like flexibility and problem solving. Nothing is perfect, of course, and you don't need to fulfil some notion of a 'perfect unschooling parent'. You do need to be willing to be actively involved, present and available for your child.

Thinking about what you want for your child now and in the future

No one can promise you what the future holds. No one can say that if you do X now with your child then it will mean Y will happen when they are older. What we can do is consider what you would like their life to look like, now and in the future. The following activities help to focus your attention on what *your* values are and to consider *your* child and their experience. I would also like to suggest, if you have a partner or co-parent, to look at these questions separately and then to discuss them together.

PAUSE AND REFLECT

Activity One

This activity invites you to consider how you came to unschooling, what events or experiences brought you to this point. They might be practical things or ideas you have about how life, childhood or education should be.

- What has led you to consider unschooling?

  ....

- What was your own educational experience like?

  ....

- Have your ideas about life, childhood or education changed? If so, how?

  ....

Activity Two

This is a space to reflect on your current situation and refine your thoughts about life and learning. If it is difficult to think about these things in terms of what you believe, or concrete ideas, consider answering these questions by thinking about what you don't want.

- What would you like your child's day-to-day experience to be like?

  ....

- What are your current hopes for your child?

  ....

- What is education for?

  ....

You can use your answers to Activity One to help you consider your long-term goals as well as to think about what that might look like on a day-to-day basis. Can you rephrase some of the answers you have written into phrases that express what you would like your child's life to look like, both now and in the future?

Here are some answers I hear frequently:

I want my child to not feel the pressure of homework, tests, attendance – I want my child to be happy and to know that their worth is not based on exam results.

I want my child to not be worried and anxious about school – I want my child's physical and mental wellbeing to be considered.

I don't want my child to feel like they are failing all the time – I want my child to experience competence and be proud of what they can and are doing without judgement.

I don't want my child to be afraid to go to the toilet – I want my child to be able to go to the toilet when they want to.

I don't want my child to be known as the naughty one – I want my child to know that they are accepted and loved just as they are.

I don't want my child to be ignored when they are upset – I want my child to be cared for and nurtured.

I don't want my child to be forced to choose a career and narrow down their choices before they are ready – I want my child to grow up and contribute to the world in a meaningful way that is fulfilling for them.

My child lost the light in their eyes and was bored at school – I want my child to be interested in what they are doing and be passionate about learning.

HOPES AND DREAMS

Using your thoughts from the previous activity, write down some principles for day-to-day interactions and experience of life. Then write down some long-term goals and hopes for your life without school in the future.

Principles for day-to-day interactions and experience of life:

1. ....

2. ....

3. ....

Long term goals and hopes for the future:

1. ....

2. ....

3. ....

These are not hard and fast targets for you to stick to. As you will discover as you read on, there is lots of room for exploration and discovery, for changing your mind and making changes, and that includes adapting as your understanding deepens and as your children grow. It might even be that you return and redo this activity once you finish reading this book. It is a fluid exercise and open to being rethought.

A whole new world

School isn't fit for children; children are made to fit into school. Over the years the expectations have become higher, and earlier, especially in the UK. It used to be that the primary school curriculum was based on enquiry and exploring – if you read the National Curriculum in the UK you might actually find yourself surprised to find that it is largely focused on skills development. Curriculums break down knowledge and content into a day-by-day plan, and it is common for schools across the nation to teach the same topics within the same year groups, at the very same hour. School is a problem.

Unschooling questions everything that parents know about living and learning. When you first hear about it, it can be a little bit like pulling the rug out from under your feet. What is this? How on earth does it work? What exactly do we do? It is my intention that this book answers those questions for you and equips you to start your journey into unschooling.

My one piece of enduring advice that I would encourage you to carry with you throughout this book and beyond is to **start with the ideas that make sense to you**. Unschooling is not like changing your brand of cereal or, in educational terms, swapping to a different curriculum. You shouldn't do things purely because I say this is it or you read somewhere else that that is the unschooling answer. Always take time to think through what that might look like for your family, how it can be implemented in a way that benefits you all and brings around change for the better.

Second to that would be to **take your time to make changes** (even when they make sense to you). Even if the ideas make sense for you, take a pause before overhauling your child's life and making any big changes. It can seem exciting, and you might be keen to get started, but you have time to make changes slowly and with consideration. Learning is a lifelong process; there is no impending deadline of doom or set point at which success or failure is declared and taints your child's record for the rest of their life. Spend this time discovering more about unschooling, read the recommended books, follow these interviewed families online, and spend time reacquainting yourself with your children. Love and nurture them as they recover from school and do things together that they enjoy.

The further you move away from school practices, **the more you drop schooled ways, the closer you get to unschooling**. The joy and success of unschooling lies in the fact that it is not school in every way possible.

Principles to live by

- Children are natural learners.
- Start with the ideas that make sense to you.
- Take your time to make changes.
- The more you drop schooled ways, the closer you get to unschooling.

Chapter 2

Neurodiversity and the Need for Something Different

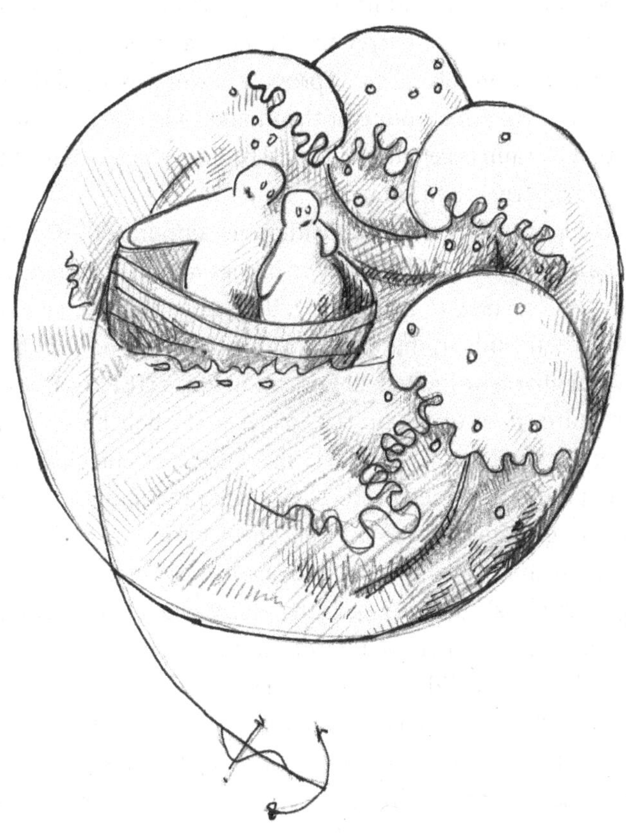

Did you read the title of the first chapter? It said, 'When school is a problem'. And I talked about some of the ways that school is problematic. School. Not you. And not your child.

There are many children who find school intensely difficult. It's not their fault. School wasn't built for children, and it certainly wasn't built for these children. These are the children who cannot and will not comply. These are the children who cannot and will not conform. These are the children who are telling us loud and clear that something is wrong. These are the children who urge us to consider something different and herald in another way for learning to happen.

In schools these children are seen as disruptive and labelled as 'problematic'. They get in the way of others paying attention and learning. They don't fit the norm and become a blot on school ratings. They require 'additional support': resources and staffing. Some schools are better than others at meeting individual needs. Some geographical areas provide better provision than others for those who don't quite fit the mould. Wherever you are, it is likely that the aim is getting your child to access school with a focus on improving their behaviour.

It is highly likely that a considerable amount of effort is put into coaching your child on how to access mainstream education. The focus is on how to help your child change their behaviours or improve their skills so that they can fit in. This can be seen in their behaviour charts or Individual Education Plans (IEPs) with targets that require them to: sit on the carpet with their hands in their laps; look at the person who is talking to them; attend class with all the equipment that they need. The goal is predominantly focused on how to get this child to do what the school wants them to do. The responsibility is on the child to change, and in this way (and in many other ways) the message is that it is your child who is at fault.

What happens when we flip this narrative on its head? What if we said that your child is doing the best that they can and that the behaviours they are displaying are telling you something? What if we know that they are developmentally right where they are supposed to be, and that there is no rush or pressure to be anywhere else? What if we stopped trying to change our children to fit into a standardised box and we did something else instead? What would happen if the education was changed to suit your child?

Listening to our young people

I would like to introduce you to two young people who are going to share their experiences of school with you, how they came to home education, and what their lives look like now. Their stories are personal and theirs to tell, but they are echoed in varying renditions across the home-educating community (and I am certain in other places too).

Please welcome Jess. Jess is 11 years old and has been unschooled for two years. She left mainstream school during Year 4 after finding herself unable to tolerate or understand the rules and finding it hard to sit still for hours at a time. After trying various interventions and attempts to support her in school, she was deregistered and began unschooling. After leaving school Jess has forged her own way and is happily learning without school.

You will also be hearing from Chloe. Chloe is currently 16 years old and can be found advocating for positive teen authenticity and neurodiversity at Me Just Me. She left mainstream school at the age of seven, after finding that the teachers and environment were unable to accommodate her. During our conversation together she explained how the teachers didn't 'fully understand' and were not 'well versed in Chloe'. She was able to articulately express to teachers how demeaning the accommodations that they did make made her feel. She found they often did not know how to respond to a young child challenging their authority in any way. After leaving school, Chloe has thrived within the flexibility and personalised approach that home education has been able to provide.

Young people who don't fit into the school system express this in different ways. It is often their behaviour that is telling us that something is wrong, not that their behaviour is, or that they are, wrong. Children often melt down, mask, shut down or stand up. What every child and young person needs in this world is someone on their side, someone who will listen to them and hear what they are saying through their words and their actions. Your child is not at fault, and neither are you.

It is a radical act in our society to listen to your child, to include them in the discussions about their life, and what is happening to them and how they are experiencing the world. It is an act that will change you and your child's world for the better. So sit back and listen to Jess and Chloe as they share their experiences and articulate what many of our children can't but desperately need us to hear.

Making sense of it all

School takes effort. Getting up in the morning, putting on a uniform, being ushered from pillar to post: class to class, lesson to lesson, assembly, playtime, PE, wash your hands, tie up your hair, line up here, walk on the left, 'This is what we are learning today', 'This is what we are learning today', 'This is what we are learning today', finish this page, paint this picture, list those properties, sit down, look at the teacher, put up your hand, and don't talk. And when you have done all of that, then you get to go home and do your homework. If you get these things right, you're seen to be doing well.

Some children find it easy to comply and others excel at it: listening to instructions, remembering the rules and controlling their emotions and behaviours. For others it takes significantly more effort. The instructions can be too complex, the rules don't make sense and they aren't developmentally ready to manage their own emotions independently. And when the effort they put in doesn't match the set expectations, it can fall apart. This is interpreted as poor behaviour.

Jess explained in her interview:

> " I never liked the rules because they didn't really make sense to me. Why did they make up rules? Like the uniforms: the shoes were really annoying in the summer. They get warm and tight, and I just want to take them off, but you're not allowed to. You have to wear their socks, which I didn't understand either. Why can't you wear your own socks?

Sometimes the effort children put in all day means that the falling apart happens at home. There is no time for homework. There is only time for crying, watching TV or bubbly baths. This can mean hours of recovery and exhaustion from the effort of 'being good', trying to fit in and play the game so that they can win too or simply not stand out.

Even for those children who are supported in school their experiences vary wildly, and there is always an undertone that the child should be doing and accessing the same things as everyone else. The ultimate goal is to have the young person back in school and back in class.

Jess told me about how this made her feel:

> "I had a wellbeing session before school. We did colouring or craft or something that was really nice. Sometimes I only stayed in for that and never stayed in for the rest of school. I'm not sure they really liked it. There was one week when I was only doing the colouring in the wellbeing sessions and not going to school. They said that I needed to go into school for most of the day. The problem was, if I was off for a few days, they would say that I need to go into school but it's actually harder to go to school when they pressured me.

A huge amount of effort goes into playing the game that is school, and once upon a time, you might have thought that it was energy spent on the right thing for your child. That striving to do it all was in fact helping and supporting your child in the best way you could, the best way possible. Even to the extent of doing what the school told you, despite your child's objections, and behaviours and health declining.

One of the problems with the approach that school takes is that children are not robots. They are human beings, each one complex and unique. There are many factors that affect a young person's learning. You can't programme in a target, or expectation, or even set out a learning objective for a particular lesson and expect a child to focus solely on that and forget other things occurring in their lives. Lives are multifaceted, and children's attention, and capacity for academic learning, may be influenced by any manner of things: tiredness, hunger, noise levels, inactivity, the death of a pet, a lost toy, unwell family members, worrying news reports or, like Jess, wearing uncomfortable shoes. Many a thing can have an impact on any child that will affect their mood, physical comfort and ability to concentrate fully on the task set by a teacher.

Chloe shared some of her frustrations with school, how she experienced a lack of consideration for individuality and the push towards compliance:

> School didn't work for starters, because lots of the teachers weren't well versed in Chloe. Even the teachers who understood didn't really fully understand either. There were things put in place to more suit their needs than mine. There was stuff like the 'Chloe circle', which I had to sit in so I could fidget in that circle, because they didn't want me disrupting other kids from fidgeting. I understood that that was demeaning, and I was actually very good at articulating that. I used to go up to the teachers and explain to them how 'it feels quite demeaning for you to reduce me to a circle', and then they wouldn't know how to respond to a five-year-old who could articulate that well. They don't actually know how to cope with the fact that a child is holding them up on how they act.
>
> We had a lot of issues in the system, swimming was one of them. I didn't want to go in a deep pool, because I was stressed in water. I could only go in shallow pools with armbands, and I did not like getting water in my eyes, nose, face, hair, anything. That's stressful for me. But they used to teach kids by pushing them in the pool. I managed to get to stay home from swimming practice because of how much I just got stressed. I wrote a letter to them explaining how I did not want to go to swimming practice and about infringement of human rights at age seven.
>
> I find a lot of kids are taught from a very young age that the teachers, parents, adults have the authority, so whatever they say goes. And then kids don't actually have the capacity to think, 'Well, why can't I question them?' All they get told is, if you question, you get told off, or you get this revoked, and you are punished. You don't get the reason

> why you can't question anything. There is no good reason why you shouldn't question things. I got that a lot in school, because I was a very big questioner. I questioned everything. 'Why?' And the one thing I hated most, and that I got told most of my early life is, 'Because I said so'. That is the worst phrase in human history, nothing about why.

No more striving to fit in

What unschooling proposes isn't programmes that separate children from their peers, spotlight their difficulties or impress targets on them for the benefit of the school system. It's a whole new approach. **Unschooling centres your child.** It radically accepts, embraces and celebrates who they are, and freely gives them the support that they need until they naturally move on in their own time.

Unschooling is an invitation to put your energy into nurturing the whole child. It is possible to cease striving to reach all these markers: developmental milestones, age-appropriate expectations, learning targets. You can stop putting your time and effort into achieving what others have set as goals for your child and turn your energy towards your child. Unschooling is an educational approach that allows you to partner your child. To come alongside your child, truly listen to their words, thoughts and feelings, understand their behaviours, and include their health, mental, emotional and physical wellbeing in the equation. It enables all facets of a person to be considered, not diminishing or sacrificing one aspect for the gain of another.

This process often begins by listening to your child and to yourself. Many parents innately know that school isn't working or isn't the place for their child to thrive. Trusting yourself and trusting that your child knows when something isn't right is counter-cultural. Professionals are full of advice and warnings about the pitfalls of not doing what they recommend, not being in school or how they know what your child needs. It can be nerve-wracking to ignore them. Terrifying even. Unschooling asks you to **trust your child**.

Here is what I know. I know my children. I have spent the longest time with my children. I relate to my children in a completely different way to anyone else on this planet. I know what makes each of them tick, I know what lights their fire, I know what worries them, I know when they shine and thrive, and I know what their needs and wants are. Okay, so I don't always know, but my focus on their wellbeing, my collective knowledge about them from all aspects of their life, and my ongoing relationship with them means that I know them significantly better than anyone else, except what they know about themselves. This makes me, and you, the expert in the room on our children. And if you don't feel like that is the case, there are sections in this book that talk exclusively about recovery, repair and restoring those relationships (see Chapters 4 and 10). For now, it's time to divert your energy towards listening to your child and trusting when they say what works, or often, to begin with, what is not working for them. Table 2.1 proposes a few schooled ideas that you can move away from and what you can do instead as you create a new way forward.

Table 2.1. Creating a new way forward

Moving away from:	Moving towards:
How I can get my child to learn X	Creating a life where your child is able to learn in ways that suit them
Anxiety and shame brought on by pressure and expectations	Accepting your child just as they are
Focusing on the things that they can't do	Doing more of the things they can do and doing those things with joy
People, places and spaces that raise anxiety	Forming relationships and creating spaces that bring ease and belonging

Chloe shared with me the difference that it made having someone who listened to her at home:

> “I didn't have people misunderstanding me. It's only my mum. And it's very easy to talk to your mum and say, 'Hey, Mum, this isn't working, or this is working', and then for your mum to listen because you're her child. My mum would know not to push me in a pool, or to give a Chloe circle, or to limit what books I read.

The surprising truth is that children don't need us to tell them what to learn. What unschooling invites us to do is to create a life in which learning can flourish and grow. For children who need something different, this means that we spend significantly more time on aspects that do not look academic at all, and when they do engage in activities, it often looks completely different to how others participate. Unschooling provides an opportunity to focus on your child, who they are and what they need, and to put your effort into truly nurturing them rather than trying to fit them into a standardised box.

Jumping ship

I went white water rafting once. Just once, never again! The group started the day with the instructions and safety talk, as you can imagine. This included how to operate the raft and what to do if you fell in the river, accompanied with some information about the specific currents of this river and how to help others get back into the boat. We sailed smoothly down the first rapid. We were then catapulted from the boat on the second rapid, which I assume was deliberate so that we could put into practice the things we had been told only moments before. I hated it. I opted to spend the rest of the day travelling in the safety boat alongside one of the other participants, an instructor and a trainee. We travelled the same route but took the smooth path and someone else did the rowing for us all day.

What children need more than anything else is a safety boat and a safety crew. Life is not sink or swim. They don't have to learn to ride the rapids, work as a team, understand the rules of the river, be thrown from the boat and plunged into a slip stream and reach the end triumphant, if they're not ready to. It's actually a better idea to ride in the safety boat with the safety crew, grow in confidence on the water, get to know the river, how to operate a boat down it, and get to know the people who are travelling with you, when the challenge before you is overwhelming.

Choosing to leave school behind you and not do what seems to be working for everyone else isn't a sign that you have failed in any way. Being able to purposefully walk away from a system that is not working for your child and intentionally walk towards something new is a sign of strength. Leaving school behind may mean that you find an education that suits your child.

The safety crew

What Chloe inadvertently did when I interviewed her was to pick up on one of the key elements that makes a significant difference to children, their lives and learning.

What your child needs more than a reading programme, reward system, daily balancing exercises or spotlighting their difficulties is a safe person. One person who is on their side, one person who knows them as well as they know themself, one person who walks with them through this world and helps them to navigate it. One safe person.

From this single safe relationship life is smoother and easier to navigate. Physical needs can be met, co-regulation is at hand, facilitating sensory or other neurological preferences is easier. Most importantly it means providing your child with a positive experience of core relationships, someone who is consistent, secure, someone who listens to them, loves them and accepts them for who they are. **You are their advocate and their partner**.

Having a safe person means that children get to experience an anchor in what can often be a very stormy world. Having someone they can hang on to, someone they can trust, someone who consistently shows up and someone who does not abandon them. Being in an emotionally safe relationship means being able to share all facets of themselves without hiding, pretending or being performative for the benefit of behavioural points, test scores or approval. Being able to authentically be who they are, their joys, their personal expression, as well as be valued and cared for through dysregulation or other human struggles.

The safety boat

Feeling comfortable and safe often means having a place where you can relax, be yourself and do whatever you need to do. For children who are 'fine when they are at school', only to get home and strip all their clothes off and run screaming around the house, this is because home is a safe place for them. Children need a physical place of safety, one that is theirs and there if they need it. It could include their favourite toys, games, blankets, sensory aids. It might be a home-made den, pop-up tent, their bed, a whole room or the car. A place that is private, away from everyone and everything else.

This space needs to be readily and consistently available. For some children, knowing that the space is there for them to return to when they need to is what enables them to venture out beyond it. These things take time, though, and in the beginning you may find that a significant amount of time is spent building and establishing these places of safety.

This approach is a complete U-turn from a schooled approach – the nurturing of our young people, creating the right environment for them, providing support along the way and allowing them to unfold in their own time.

The safety kit

One of the simplest and yet most effective ways of making a difference to your child's life is to lean into their needs and preferences and give them the things that make them feel more physically comfortable, safe and regulated, and to do it with abandon.

Just like the flowers in a garden, your child is a unique and beautiful individual. Every child has their own ebb and flow and their own set of care instructions. Granted, unlike a plant they don't come with an instruction label and they are likely to change, but, just like the plants in a garden, they each need to have their own needs met, otherwise their growth will be affected.

FREE TO BE THEMSELF

In this exercise I invite you to consider some of the basic physical needs that humans have, to think about your child's current preferences, and consider how they can be met.

First, draw a plant or a flower in a box in the centre of a piece of paper. It doesn't have to be perfect, and you don't have to do it at all! It really doesn't even matter what it looks like. If you are apprehensive, one way to approach this is to complete the drawing without the pencil leaving the paper. It really is just for fun and to enable you to take a moment between thinking about all these ideas and forming them into some order.

Second, I want you to consider what this plant or flower needs, remembering that it represents your child. Around the outside of your drawing, make notes under different headings:

- Consider your child's hydration needs. What is their preferred drink? Do they have a special cup or bottle that they like? Do they actively remember to get their own drinks when they need them, or do you need to make them readily available?

- What does your child like to eat? What are their favourite foods? Are there places where they find it easier to eat than others? Are there certain conditions under which eating is easier? Are they able to say when they are hungry, or do you need to provide easy access to food and be attentive to their hunger cues?

- How does your child respond to physical touch? What fabrics do they like? Do they have favourite clothes or bedding? Do they enjoy holding hands or a hand on their back? Do they respond well to deep pressure and rough play? Are they sensitive to touch or do they avoid it?

- Does your child have clear wake-and-rest cycles? Do they have a regular high-energy time? Do they have more settled, restful or sleepy times of the day that you need to consider allowing for? Can they recognise their own sleep cues, or do you need to provide support towards needed restful times?

- How much space or social contact does your child need to be nourished? Are they focused on who they are seeing today rather than on what they are doing, or do they currently show little interest in forming relationships with peers? Are they able to engage with others under certain conditions? Who are those people and what are the conditions? How can you create time for these preferences to be catered for?

Lean into the practical things that make your child's life better. Take their favourite teddy bear everywhere with them. Put their drink in the blue cup and not another one. Have their favourite food stocked up in the cupboard. Spend hours lining up the toy cars. Have their clothes of choice ready and available. Find places where they can run, roll, climb and spin freely. Provide cosy spaces where they can rest whenever they need to and give them the freedom to go to the toilet when they need to (it's incredibly disappointing that this one is even in the list, but there it is).

Togetherness and ease

What we see happen, right from the beginning, is a shift from striving to coming to a place of ease. The more we resisted driving their learning, by setting expectations and our efforts being placed in cajoling them via various means, which strained our day-to-day interactions, the easier it became for the children to freely engage in the activities of their choice. As we set aside striving for the next milestone, and truly put energy into working with our children, **we created a supportive environment** for our children to confidently explore the world around them and learn what they need to, when they need to (see Figure 2.1).

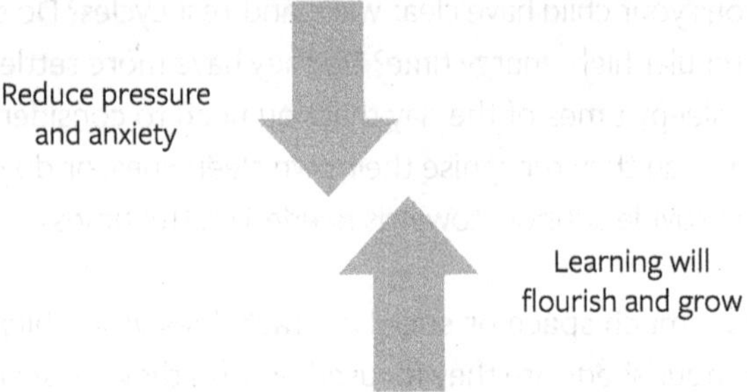

Figure 2.1. Reduce pressure and anxiety

Jess explained to me the things she does now that the arbitrary rules of school and the expectations have been removed from her life. Remember as you read this that this is two years after she has left school and after two years of unschooling:

> I've figured out what interests I have. Whereas at school I didn't have an interest in anything. And it just felt a little bit boring.
>
> I can do drama. I do tap and other dances on a Saturday. And if I was in school, I wouldn't have done them even though they're a Saturday because it would have been too tiring. I recently had a Tap Show, and I wouldn't have done that if I was in school. I really enjoyed it. Some of the clubs that I go to are in the middle of the day, so I couldn't have done them when I was at school and I would have missed out on the fun stuff.

As well as giving children the opportunity to engage with life in a meaningful way, it enables them to do it their way. To explore the world in ways that excite them, in ways that they can relate to, in ways that are smooth and enjoyable, and in their own space and time.

Chloe shared with me how she was able to take her time and come to things when she was ready:

> I was really struggling to do things, choosing to do things. My mum had this brilliant approach called 'Setting things up on the table'. She would pretend to do them, or do a bit of them. She did the activities

to make it look interesting. I would look at them and go, 'No, I don't want to do that'. Then I would wander around the house for about an hour, and then I'll go, 'Well, I have to find out. I have to figure out what this is on the table'. Then I join in and eventually have fun.

Being in the right boat, with the right people, on the right river

It's not that we don't think about the learning that is happening but that the learning isn't the goal anymore. The goal is to create an environment in which learning can flourish and grow for your child. The aim is to reduce anxiety and pressure by centring your child and providing what they need to be at ease with themself. Learning happens more effectively and consistently when our brains are not in a state of flight or fright (survival mode) and the nervous system is regulated. When our brains are not in survival mode, they are able to put effort and energy into learning, acquiring new information and sorting it and connecting it to information we already have. This is made significantly more difficult if you are living in a state of distress or being asked to behave in ways or to do things you are unable to do.

Some of the changes you make need not be that big, but they do make a big difference – simple ideas like:

- Your child can now use the toilet at the point when they need to.

- They can eat when they need to (be warned – children are natural grazers and are not programmed to eat three meals a day with snacks in between! Your food bill is likely to increase!).

- Being able to wear clothes that they are comfortable in, even when they leave the house. I wish I could show you the photo I have of my four-year-old sitting on her pink scooter wearing a maroon t-shirt with a digger on it, pink leggings, one camouflage welly boot, one pink welly boot, a tutu and swimming googles on her head, ready for a trip out.

- Simply being able to rest or even sleep when they need to, more downtime, more processing time, more physical rest for those who need it – this has an impact on how they are then able to engage with things when they are awake as well as removing the stress of performing and inducing feelings of failure.

- Learning to listen to your body and providing what it needs so that it is better equipped to do what it can when it can is a simple but impactful change that can be made when your child is not in school.

By focusing on your child, providing them with safety, with a space in which they are free to be themselves and that meets their needs right now in this moment, you are creating a life in which learning can happen with ease. That doesn't mean that it is easy! This is only the first step and it is a pretty big one as it turns its back on almost everything that mainstream school has probably advised you. Having lived this life for 18 years now I know that it is not a magic wand, but I also know that treating young people with respect and listening to them has made a difference to how they see themselves and how they interact with the world for the better.

Principles to live by

- Centre your child.
- Trust your child.
- Be your child's advocate and partner.
- Create a supportive environment.

Chapter 3

A New Way to Live and Learn

When you need to figure out something new, like complete a tax return, fix some clothing, build a chicken coop or take up any new pastime, how do you go about doing it?

A few years ago, I decided that I wanted to learn to crochet. I had been a knitter for over 20 years, but I was drawn to the patterns, colours and textures of crocheted items and wanted to learn how to do it. As I knew how to work with wool, I figured that it would be an easy step to take. I had recently been using YouTube videos to discover different recipes for cooking, so my first port of call was to look for tutorials on YouTube. My brain exploded. First, I was overwhelmed with all the options. However, I did manage to narrow it down to ones that were listed as 'easy'. It was quite a comical experience. After watching a video several times before even starting, spending a significant amount of time setting up the wool in one hand and attaching it to the hook in the other, it was clear that this was going to be more complicated than I had thought. I persevered. The real turning point came when I tried to begin the process of crocheting with the wool wrapped as it should be around one hand, the hook held in the other and attached to the wool, watching what I was doing, and simultaneously watching the 'easy tutorial'. It was disastrous. I needed to pause and skip back certain sections multiple times and needed a slow-motion option, but all that is difficult when your hands are tied up with wool.

My interest in crochet had been piqued by having several friends who crocheted items. I told some of them that I was giving it a go and shared the tale of the easy video tutorials. It might seem logical here that they would offer to show me how to get started, but it is quite rare for me to accept others telling me what to do. What they were able to do, that helped me get started, was twofold. One of them found a 'crochet for beginners' book in a second hand shop, purchased and gifted it to me. I still have this book now and use it frequently. It has photos and clear written instructions that don't move when you are learning a stitch. Another friend recommended a blog site for tutorials and patterns. Again, I still follow and crochet items from this site regularly. The written descriptions, still pictures and glorious finished items are all fabulous.

These days I would say that I am competent at crochet. I know how to crochet a range of basic stiches, and I have successfully made blankets, toys and clothing items. I'm not perfect, though, or an expert. I often have wobbly edges on straight-edged items, I am constantly counting my stitches if I want my item to follow a pattern accurately, and I frequently make mistakes. But I learned a new skill, without someone else telling me that I had to, or forcing me to continue learning in a format that wasn't working for me. YouTube worked for cooking dinner, not for crochet tutorials.

There are lots of different ways to learn something new. Following instructions on a video, through a manual or being shown by a knowledgeable other. Observing others for a while before doing it yourself or jumping in at the deep end and just doing it. You can break a task down into small steps and master each step as you go, or you can take the whole picture and begin on it as a whole. You can dismantle things to see how they work and then get the parts or tools you need as you progress, or you can research that all beforehand and get things ready before you take it apart. You can listen to podcasts, or go to interest-led groups; you can read books about it, or physically go to a place or museum you are curious about. Watch films or documentaries. Contact others and share information online. You can spend a minute on it, a day, a year, or a lifetime.

Learning without school or a school-like approach isn't a completely foreign idea. This exercise invites you to take time to think about how you learn things now that school is not a major part of your life.

LEARNING WITHOUT SCHOOL

This is an exercise you can do with yourself in mind or with your child in mind.

I would like you to think of something that you or your child has learned without school, or without a school-like approach (e.g. classes). What was it that you or your child learned? It could be something big or small – changing a light bulb or learning to scuba dive, for example.

Now take some time to answer the following questions:

- What made you want to learn it?
- What was the first thing you did?
- What resources and materials did you use?
- Where did you find them? How did you know where to look?
- Were there other people involved? How did you know who to ask? What did they do to help you?
- How did you feel about it? Was it fun? Interesting? Useful? Boring?
- Did you find it easy or difficult to learn what you set out to learn?
- How did you keep going if it was difficult?
- Did you discover anything more than you intended to when you first set out?

As adults we adopt many ways of learning a new skill or developing an understanding of a new idea. We often get creative, compile lists, draw diagrams, take notes, talk through ideas, mull things over, get out the Post-it® notes, use voice notes, buy new stationary, invest in a coach, read a blog or book, subscribe to a kit, sign up to an introductory offer and try it out. Children, on the other hand, are exposed to only one model of learning at school, but children can learn in much the same way and in all its different permutations.

Some children prefer to follow instructions, like when they receive a LEGO model and it comes with an instruction booklet. They are happy to sit and work through it until they have built the completed item. Even then some prefer to line up all the pieces before they start and check them all, while others find the correct pieces as they go. Others want to try building it without using the instructions, while others still don't want a prepackaged model – they would prefer to free build with a selection of random LEGO bricks and figure it out for themselves.

Some children enjoy discovering how things work by taking them apart and examining the insides. Others prefer a labelled diagram from a book, a walk-through video or a documentary. Some children like to feel confident in their abilities before starting while others dive in without any prior knowledge or experience. There are numerous ways to learn, and children don't stick to just one method all the time. It's not as simple as identifying the one way in which a child learns; various approaches can be utilised within a single project. By recognising and embracing this plethora of learning styles, and creating space for them all to be explored and used as your child sees fit, we create the possibility that learning can flow and happen with ease.

Unschooling is not an entirely unfamiliar concept to us when we apply it to our own adult lives and learning. What we are not familiar with is seeing children in the driving seat of their own lives and learning.

Many researchers have written papers about how self-directed education works, the aspects that underpin its success, the long-term prospects of children who are unschooled, and other discussions. Advocates have declared its benefits for decades, and there are numerous blogs, podcasts and websites that discuss the realities of unschooling and champion families across the world. It might seem like a new idea to some, but there is a whole host of others out there embracing a life without school, and children happily living and learning as they go.

You have the pleasure of reading the experiences of other unschooling families here. We heard from Jess and Chloe in the previous chapter, but I am going to introduce all the families to you now (including Jess and Chloe) so that you have a single point of contact to remind you of who they are, what their family set-up is, how long they have been unschooling, and to hear their unschooling story in their own words.

Name: Chloe

Links

Facebook: www.facebook.com/chloemejustme

Instagram: www.instagram.com/chloemejustme

Ko-fi: https://ko-fi.com/atlasdoodles

Introduction

Chloe from Me Just Me advocates for positive authenticity and neurodiversity. She uses her online space to advocate, bring awareness and understanding surrounding home education, PDA (pathological demand avoidance) and autism.

> “I started home education at the age of seven and that was because the school environment was not accepting of my autism and were not adapting to my needs. I enjoyed my self-led learning journey as I got to have the freedom to be myself and learn the way that worked for me, I have had many adventures and experiences and I have the confidence to pursue my dreams. I agreed to share my story as I want others to know there is always another way.

Name: Nicola

Links

YouTube: https://youtu.be/TtX4s-fSHLw?si=LI_IpDe-jgDTgNCD

Introduction

> “I live in rural Oxfordshire with my son (now 19) and daughter (now 16). I turned to home education out of desperation after my son's accident and traumatic return to school, and this soon unfolded into an unschooling story. My son has been unschooled for 10 years, and my daughter enrolled at college aged 15, after nine years unschooling. My family needed a therapeutic lifestyle after trauma and I followed a path of learning and discovery. The unschooling path we followed ebbed and flowed and we developed a tight family unit who love and trust each other. I am convinced that a slow and meandering childhood is healthy for childhood development, respecting the rights of children to learn at their own pace and in their own way.

Name: Nici

Links

Author of Reality Vs Expectation (Facebook): www.facebook.com/share/1EKgGSD4Gq

Introduction

“ We are a neurodivergent unschooling family of six, from Southampton, Hampshire. We've been unschooling for over a decade, and with three of the children now post education age at 16, 17 and 21, we have just one unschooler left who is currently 11 and has never been to school. We found unschooling early in our journey, due to the older children's school-based trauma, and it quickly became a complete way of life that sat beautifully with our parenting views and ideals. We were aiming for family principles of 'Happy, healthy, respected and connected', and unschooling exemplifies that and so much more.

Name: Sally

Introduction

“ Our family consists of myself, my partner and our three children: our eldest son (18), a son (16) and a daughter (12). We have been home educating and unschooling for several years. The older two left formal schooling when they were around 10 and 9 years old, respectively, while our daughter has never attended a traditional school. They initially attended an alternative playgroup and later spent approximately three to four years at a very alternative school. However, the model did not fully meet our needs. Consequently, we have been pursuing home education for about eight to nine years.

Name: Sarah

Links

Facebook: www.facebook.com/sarah.beale1
The Renegade Mum: www.renegademum.com

Introduction

Sarah currently lives in Australia with her four children, two of whom have never been to school. They have spent the last several years travelling and living in the UK and Europe, using an educational and lifestyle philosophy known as 'worldschooling' – really just a variation of home educating that focuses on being in the world and engaging with it in a holistic way. They returned home recently to 'plug back in' and plan to continue their travels later.

Sarah was also somewhat sceptical of the school system, or at least became so after having her first child in 2008. She became, first, concerned about what school would do to her young child's creativity, which was evident every day, and then, curious about what else children might learn, independently, and without formal teaching. It would be several years before her family took the leap away from school. Ultimately, the reasons for ditching school weren't specifically philosophical or political (although they have become more so in recent years!) but based on the kind of lifestyle Sarah wanted to lead with her family. Thankfully her husband was on the same page and has always been supportive of the choice to educate and live without school, and they immediately embraced 'unschooling'.

Sarah agreed, very readily, to contribute to this book as an offering to the wider unschooling community. Eldership supported her to have felt confident to make this choice with her family, and sharing stories with others is an important part of strengthening communities. Having other families with whom to walk this unconventional path is crucial in building not only relationships that support the learning of our children, but practically creates a support network and scaffolding for living.

Name: May Ling and Steve

Links

May Ling Thomas: www.maylingthomas.com

Introduction

May Ling and Steve live with their two daughters in East London. They heard about unschooling through an attachment parenting group. Seeing their children growing and learning spontaneously, it just made sense not to impose adult expectations and restrictions on their children – or themselves! They agreed to share their experiences because unschooling inspired them to make much bigger changes to the way they live. They now weave work into their unschooling lives, Steve in classical music and May Ling as a coach, healer, facilitator and organiser.

Name: Sorrel

Introduction

Sorrel lives with their wife and two children aged 11 and 5. They came to home education and unschooling following their early experiences of nursery with their eldest child. They visited one nursery where the children were strapped down into chairs as they ate, even though the chairs were close to the floor. Sorrel doesn't recall even trying this nursery. When they tried another nursery when their eldest child was 2½, they left him a couple of times to try to settle him in. The nursey staff said that he was doing great and doing fine. One day they were walking home and their son told them that there was a lot of crying and they asked their son, 'Who was crying?' and he said 'Oh, me' and Sorrel immediately knew that the nursey was lying because their son was 2½ and 'He wouldn't be lying about that'. From that point on they knew that they wouldn't be sending their child to school.

Name: Rebecca

Introduction

“ We are a family of four living in North London. Our path into unschooling was a combination of disillusionment with schooling (particularly behaviourism), healing from personal trauma, and recognising neurodivergence in the family. Our children started in mainstream school, but their zest for life slowly evaporated in school, and during Covid I started listening to Akilah Richards' *Fare of the Free Child* podcast. Personally, I started looking at all the ways power had broken me in my life, and started to look at the minutiae of power imbalances between adults and children. From what I've seen among the unschoolers I know, once you've made this shift to 'power with' there is no going back. Your heart shifts, and everything shifts with it.

Name: Alice

Introduction

“ I live with my husband and two daughters in Croydon. My eldest daughter, 14, attends school and is currently working on GCSEs. My youngest, 12, is in her third year of unschooling. We learned about unschooling at a time when she was finding it impossible to attend school for much more than an hour a day. It felt like the perfect fit for a child who struggled with the constant demands of school.

I love being able to use my energy and focus on connecting with my child and helping her to follow her interests and passions. Unschooling has made a tremendous difference to my daughter's mental health and self-confidence, and the whole family is better for it.

Name: Jess

Introduction

“Hi. My name is Jess. I am 11 years old. I went to school from Nursery to Year 4, so six years. I was nine when I left. I really liked seeing my friends every day and the fact that I didn't need to come up with something every day, but I hated all of the rules and that you have to sit there for six hours doing work and stuff and you can't even stand up when you do work. I live with my parents and older sister in South London and I've been unschooled for two years.

Name: Susan

Introduction

“We are a family of now four, but for many years I was a single parent to two autistic PDA children, and we live in West Sussex. My eldest was in school for three years, which proved disastrous. I took him out to home educate, firmly believing we would spend some time healing and then pick up a semi-structured approach (because this best suited me). I was highly sceptical about unschooling at this point. However, it became evident that while I might want to have a semi-structured approach, this was not what my eldest needed. I had to completely change tack, learn about and embrace unschooling, and make this a whole life change. We have never looked back and have continued this approach family wide. I wanted to share our story to show people that there is a different way to learn, especially for children who are pressure-sensitive and who have challenges with compliance to external guidance/leads/instruction.

Formal learning in schools

Mainstream schools use an empty vessel model for learning. Children are perceived to be eager and waiting empty vessels ready to be filled with the glorious knowledge that the keepers of the kingdom hold. Teachers hold this knowledge and pour it into the vessels in increments controlled by them and according to a predesigned curriculum. In this way, it is understood that all children should learn roughly the same thing, at the same time as their peers (because for this process to happen, children are segregated into same-age peer groups). Children have very little say over what they learn, when and how. There is often some room for differing abilities and lessons are planned with differentiation in mind, but the teacher still decides what the next steps are for those children, and what, when and how those steps should be fulfilled. The teacher is in the driving seat.

Learning predominantly happens in a classroom, and even when it is moved beyond the four walls of school, many places replicate the classroom environment or echo the teaching and learning paradigm that occurs within schools. Learning happens in clearly defined spaces, and breaks from learning, or 'playtime', are an entirely separate notion. There is a space designated for the serious business of learning and other spaces are allocated for the 'frivolous' nature of play.

Schools also define specific learning times. Most schools operate for about six hours per day, and these are learning hours. Attendance is requested and parents and children alike are often told that every minute counts. Some schools even put up posters with calculations of missed learning minutes if your child is regularly late for school by even 10 minutes. Attendance awards are standard practice, as is homework. Homework re-enforces that learning is set by a teacher, that curriculum content is of primary importance, and that the hours matter, even if they are hours at home. Any activity that is not school-sanctioned is classed as a 'pastime' or hobby, and not as important as schoolwork.

The hidden curriculum

Most of us have been through a mainstream education system. For 12 years we have been learning more than literacy, science, the humanities or the arts. Being immersed in a system that inherently teaches us about how we learn and what makes a good learner. We carry with us beliefs and ideas about what education should look like and how children should be taught. This is known as the 'hidden curriculum', the unspoken attitudes, beliefs and norms that are taught indirectly alongside the formal curriculum. For example, 'If you work hard you will pass your exams and be successful', 'Learning topics in subject areas means that you won't have gaps in your learning', 'School teaches you everything you need to know'.

These are some of the more obvious things that we learn at school. There are a great many things that become so ingrained in our lives and our children's lives that we barely notice them until something draws our attention to it, or we catch a glimpse of something different and it challenges our thinking. We find ourselves questioning the hidden curriculum as we explore a new way of educating our children, unlearning the scripts as we truly consider what life can be like without school.

Unlearning

Just like school is not the only place for a child to be educated, school-type learning is not the only way to learn. For many this is the beginning of unlearning. The beginning of dismantling what we thought was the only way. The beginning of questioning how growth and development, gaining knowledge and skills truly happens, and happens well, and without having a detrimental effect on a child's mental, physical and emotional wellbeing. The quest to find something better or merely seeking an alternative for children who don't fit the mainstream mould. This often leads to the unlearning of all the things we have experienced in our own schooling and that have been reiterated in our child's schooling too.

Sally told me about what she thought unschooling would be like when she first set out, and how and why her thinking changed:

> “I thought that unschooling would be more about me bringing things and leading the way, so me having good ideas about things we do. I had a sense that, and I was pretty sure that, my children knew how to learn, and I didn't really doubt that. I did feel like I needed to be constantly bringing things to them and helping structure things, like I

imagine we'd be busy all day doing that. The discovery was that they needed so much more autonomy, and they were capable of so much more autonomy than I could have ever imagined, and it needed to be things that were meaningful to them. They had no desire in wasting time on things that I thought would work, but they didn't. There was zero compliance. They weren't interested in being compliant. It took me really embracing that, the autonomy piece, was really the big piece for us.

I guess I had underestimated what children are capable of. They've always been able to know what they need really, even if they haven't been able to verbalise or it has been a little bit foggy. The idea that I knew more than them, about them, has never been true. Their ability to stay connected, their ability to know what they need, their ability to learn, that blows me away. That drive they have to learn, the autonomy that a child really needs. I've been surprised at how deeply conditioned I was and how much work that took on my part. We're so used to children living without autonomy, when you see how they really can manage themselves.

Being open to the process of learning new things ourselves and exploring what works and doesn't work for our children is one of the joys as well as the challenges of unschooling. Being willing to hold lightly the things that we think that we know and make room for new ideas is an essential component to being able to unlearn and relearn.

Relearning

The unlearning is not enough, though. There must be a relearning, a replacement idea that holds well educationally. As parents we have a responsibility to 'ensure that your child of compulsory school age receives a suitable education, either by regular attendance at school or otherwise'.[1] It's not enough to let our children run wild and do whatever they want, relying on their natural ability to grow

1 Section 7, Education Act 1996: www.legislation.gov.uk/ukpga/1996/56/contents

and learn. There are things we can put in place to support their education, even when they are in the driving seat.

Unschooling is not a new concept. It is a model of education that has been around far longer than the schooling that we are familiar with. Living and learning alongside family members, within the framework of a larger community, is how children have learned and grown to be contributing members of society for thousands of years. Today's opportunities and possibilities for young people often extend beyond their immediate family, communities, and even countries. As an educational philosophy, self-directed education supports a young person's interests wherever they take them, equipping them to explore wherever and whatever they want to, as its foundations lie in nurturing lifelong learning, having a full understanding of self and being supported in their choices.

When we began home educating I knew that my children would continue learning through play for as long as they needed to. My background in child development gave me confidence in our decision to continue supporting my children's learning through their interests in LEGO, Pokémon, *Minecraft*, Barbies, painting, climbing, baking, and a great many other things they enjoyed. I saw no benefit in introducing a curriculum or trying to lure them to activities they had little interest in or resisted. Yet, I knew of no one else who was doing the same thing. No one. Not one other person on the whole planet.

I was fortunate that the first two home ed families I met with were unschooling, and as soon as I was introduced to the idea, I was able to give a name to the approach we were taking. Today I know lots of families locally who unschool their children and a great network of others across the country and around the world. It is a well-established and recognised educational philosophy practised by families across the globe.

Unschooling as a pedagogy is a cosmic shift away from our cultural experience of school. It can take a while to understand and adopt new ways of living and learning, and it is not always easy. Relearning can be intense, sometimes exciting, and other times challenging. Parents frequently find that the first year of unschooling presents the most questions. Chapter 4 takes you through the rapid adjustment process during those first few months. In the meantime, remember that it's okay to change things slowly; in fact this is preferable to changing everything at once. It's okay to have questions, and for you to seek answers. It's okay to be challenged by new ideas and to sit with feelings of uncertainty, taking your time to take things in and to move forwards slowly.

As May Ling explained in our chat together:

> “I did have a quite unrelenting ‘must do this the right way’ going on, so to think about being ‘good enough’ really helped me. Part of the choice about unschooling was about doing the best thing for our child, which was to support their autonomy, which was to give them that freedom. As time goes by, as you mellow, as you get more humble, you realise there's a benefit to only going as far as you feel comfortable. Pushing yourself to do the ideal and then exploding or blowing up and having these moments where you get angry, or where your reality is not meeting your ideal, is counterproductive.

For now, at the beginning of unschooling, let's relearn some educational ideas together:

- *Children can drive their own learning.* Humans are born naturally curious and motivated to learn; they are not empty vessels waiting to be filled. From the moment they are born, children begin to take in information from around them and respond to it. Initially babies are able to distinguish between what makes them feel safe, happy and well, and what makes them feel uncomfortable, alone or in need. In the first few years the information that children gather, interpret and integrate into their knowledge of the world is immense. It is often the time that most of us learn to do the two greatest things a human learns – to walk and to talk. These things happen without someone telling us how or giving us step-by-step instructions via daily practice. Some children learn to talk at the age of two, and others later; some find other ways to communicate altogether. The same with walking. Some children learn when they are 10 months old, others sit it out until they are 2½ years old. When the time is right, most infants find that there is a handy and trusted adult nearby to babble with them, imitate the sounds they make, sing rhymes, read stories or chatter along. The same often occurs with walking – adults make the space bigger and safer to navigate, they find walkers with wheels on for infants to push along, offer two hands for them to hold, or wait with open arms and an encouraging smile not too far away. This natural curiosity doesn't stop when your child becomes 'compulsory school age'. They don't suddenly become incapable of learning or have no idea what to learn next.

- *Learning happens everywhere and anywhere*; you do not need a specified learning space. To suggest that learning only happens when you are in a designated space with a designated teacher distracts us from the awe and wonder that surrounds us. It undermines the beauty of the world and the importance of all things. It contributes to the segregation of what is valid and valuable and what is frivolous and senseless. On the contrary, when we see the how learning can be found at the top of a tree, while paddling in a river, during a board game, in the drawing on the walls or the mixing of products in the bathroom, we can begin to feel at ease with the things our children are choosing to do.

- *Learning is happening all the time.* All activities, subjects, pastimes, events and moments are contributing to a child's understanding of the world around them. With this principle in mind, it becomes easier to see how an education is being received. The important aspect is that your child is engaged in whatever they are doing, that they are curious, exploring, questioning, observing and figuring things out. What this looks like varies enormously, and the passions, questions and pursuits of young people will also vary. Even when they are resting or appear to be relaxing, or even when they are sleeping, the brain is taking time to process new information, connect it to existing ideas, and organise it so that it makes sense.

- *Learning has no hierarchy*; whatever your child is doing, they are learning something valuable. It's not about what your child is learning, but that they are active participants in their own lives. Mainstream education has done a brilliant job at dividing the world into subject areas and listing them in order of importance. Some subjects are compulsory, some are optional, some aren't even on the timetable in some schools. You are probably familiar with the term 'core subjects', and this is reflected in forums as parents bring forth their concerns specifically regarding literacy and numeracy. The world, however, isn't divided up into subjects. **All learning is equal and connected.** Once subject dividers have been removed it can become clear how any one pursuit contributes to a deeper knowledge and understanding across a range of 'subjects'.

There are many benefits to incorporating these few principles into our children's lives and learning. Most noticeable is that their choices, abilities and interests are given value (see Table 3.1).

Table 3.1. Unschooling ideas

Children can drive their own learning	
Instead of persuading your child to participate in an activity you have chosen...	See the learning in the things they choose to do
Learning happens everywhere and anywhere	
Instead of creating a specified space for learning...	See the world as your classroom

<table>
<tr><th colspan="2">Learning is happening all the time</th></tr>
<tr><td>Instead of timetabling sessions for learning solely in 'school hours'...</td><td>Lean into natural rest and active cycles and be open to concentrated activity or deep discussions at any time of the day</td></tr>
<tr><th colspan="2">All learning is equal and connected</th></tr>
<tr><td>Instead of being interested in core subjects above other passions and pastimes...</td><td>Be equally supportive of all the things your child enjoys doing</td></tr>
</table>

Rethinking learning

Unschooling provides a unique opportunity for your child to contribute to their own life and learning, for them to be in the driving seat of their own education. It enables them to pursue the things they are good at and have a desire to discover more about, within spaces that suit their needs and alongside people who cheer them on. It centres on the child, who they are and what they need to thrive, with you being an active part of that process. In short, it is a full life without school, or the influence of school, as far as is possible. Unschooled children are getting on with the business of living, facilitated by caring and engaged adults. Their learning happens naturally as they engage with the real world around them.

Unlearning and relearning what we understand about learning and how it happens is an essential part of getting to grips with unschooling. It isn't simply about not doing school. Relearning everything we believe about learning is a long process. In the beginning there are some steep learning curves, lots of questions and fears. There are things you can practically do to remove school approaches and even schooled thinking from your home, especially in the early days. Understanding that these are replaced with ideas and approaches rather than a practical 'how to' guide to unschooling is part of the relearning.

The ideas discussed here are thoughts for you to consider and apply to your unique family situation. Unschooling is flexible and adaptable, not a one-size-fits-all. It provides a foundation for choices and decisions in our families, but only you can determine how it will work in your home. I have yet to find a family where it is not possible for unschooling to be a successful educational approach, but it does need to be intentional and adopted with purpose.

Principles to live by

- Children can drive their own learning.
- Learning happens everywhere and anywhere.
- Learning is happening all the time.
- All learning is equal and connected.

Chapter 4

The First Year Without School

The first year without school is filled with promise. The relief of not going to school again and the excitement of something new. Then, alongside that relief and excitement, there is often fear, uncertainty and guilt. It is a time filled with high expectations and a rollercoaster of emotions, and that's just the adults!

When your child physically leaves school (or moves away from school-at-home) and all school-like ways, there will be a period of adjustment. It is inevitable, especially when you are changing your learning approach. It is helpful to be able to know and say, 'We are unschooling', but there will be a time of transition between one educational experience and another. There is a cosmic shift in your life, the life of your child and your family, as you move from school to unschool.

It is highly likely that your child has had a negative experience at school, or that you have come to realise that a mainstream approach is not what you want for your child. Either of these reasons will give rise to your child needing to adjust to a new way of life without school. It can be as simple as getting used to not having to get up and be rushed in the morning, or as deep as nurturing self-belief after ongoing bullying. There are hundreds of ways in which school has moulded and impacted your child that have helped them to form beliefs and views about themselves and the world. These patterns of living and these beliefs that have formed will be challenged and changed in those first few months.

Nicola has produced a short film about their move into unschooling.[1] Her eldest son had a serious accident at the age of seven that completely changed their lives. When I spoke to Nicola about her children and their unschooling journey, she was keen to emphasise one point:

> “I'll just clarify the trauma, because we had the one major accident, but going into school for six months after the accident was repeated trauma. That was the one that compounded and complexified everything. My son didn't want to go to school at all and either me or his dad were convincing him every other day. School basically said, 'He's fine in school'. No one was listening to me. I was losing my mind, so my son was having to deal with the fact that I was completely falling apart and he was hating school. He was losing his stuff. He couldn't do any of the work. He was fighting – all things that he'd never done before the accident. He was an emotional wreck at the end of every

1 *A Freak Accident*, YouTube: https://www.youtube.com/watch?v=TtX4s-fSHLw

> day. It was absolutely awful. He started getting physical ticks and his mental state was rock bottom. He did January to July on a part-time basis. He was significantly worse going back to school after the accident than if he hadn't. That experience of school complexified his psych state completely. It was a much bigger trauma than the accident.

You might not have experienced the same situation as Nicola and her son, but maybe there are common threads in her words. She highlights things that are repeated across the unschooling community where there are many children who don't want to go to school. Can you resonate with not being listened to, school staff ignoring child and parental input and suggestions from professionals compounding an already complex situation? Your child may need to recover from their experience, but don't forget that you may need the time to recover too.

There is something magical about the moment that you have deregistered and are able to confidently say, 'You don't have to go to school again.' Even if your child has been a school refuser for a while and hasn't attended, the fact that no one is going to ask them to go releases them (and you) from the pressure and into a future of possibilities. But once the relief and the excitement wears off, what often happens next is unexpected.

It often starts with what looks like a step backwards. This is where the recovery begins for your child: doing less and cocooning more, having meltdowns and extended periods of dysregulation. Because this is the time that they can fully let go, where they reveal all the emotions and express all the stresses and pressures they have been feeling from their schooled experience. Whatever it looks like, it won't be the joyful and inquisitive life you were hoping to jump into – that bit comes later. This bit is an essential part of the process, and just like a great many other unschooling things, you can't make it better or reach the goal overnight, but you can do things that will help and support them through this time of transition.

Alongside the outpouring of emotions comes restoration – restoring both your child's sense of self and their innate ability to learn, both of which require your belief in your child and your confidence and trust in them. These are two things that school is good at stripping away from children. Simply saying, 'I believe in you' or expecting them to know what their interests are and what they want to do today isn't enough, though. They need to see your belief in them in every interaction you have. Every time you talk *with* them, every time you make a decision *with* them, valuing their input, ideas and viewpoint, these are small ways that say, 'You matter and you are important'.

Parallel to the recovery and restoration comes the recreation. This is the part where you step into a life of curiosity, fascination, awe and wonder. This is the part where your child is free to be themself and confidently explore the world on their own terms. This is the unschooling life that will be created and this is the part you are most looking forward to. It is the part that you will come to once your child has journeyed through recovery and restoration. This is the part where you will see healing and your child returning to their former self, when that spark in their eyes returns. Figure 4.1 illustrates the intricacies of this process and the constant motion between these states as your child actively recovers from their schooled experience.

***Figure* 4.1.** *The stages of recovery*

This chapter is going to focus on what to expect after you have deregistered. Everyone's school experience is different, of course, and the depths of pain and the release from the system will present themselves in different ways in different families, but a period of transition still occurs no matter what that recovery process looks like for your child. The interviews shared here are so that you can see that you are not alone and that there is a way through. Beyond poor school experiences and your child's burnout, these families show that there can be healing and a life of curiosity. This is a chapter about the initial journey from school to unschool.

Recovery: the first step

The decision to deregister your child from school is not an easy one to make and is never taken lightly. More often than I would like, I hear stories about it being a 'last resort'. That a child's experience of school is so catastrophically bad or that a school has failed to support them to such a degree that parents and children have reached breaking point.

Rebecca is a parent to two children; both are now unschooled. Her eldest daughter went to school for four years and her son for two years. Her daughter was deregistered first and then, a year later, her son:

> “My son is a super, super-sensitive kid, and he had always been very, very close to me, and school was robbing him of that sense of himself. He started refusing to go to school. And obviously the school's argument was, (a) 'He's fine in school' and (b) 'His sister's left so of course he's going to be jealous'. There was this guilt: we have to abide by these rules. I basically frog marched him in, and it was so unbearable. He ran back across the road, we were both in floods of tears at the door, and they peeled him off me. I walked home and I sobbed. I shook for two hours, and I thought, 'How am I doing this?' And 'If I feel like this, what has that done to him?' because I was in such a state at the door. I said to him, 'You never have to come back here if you don't want'.

For there to be a beginning to recovery, their needs to be an end point to schooling. The moment you deregister you step forward into something new and leave school behind you. Until that point there are always the phone calls with the school, the welfare checks, the work being sent home, the meetings and reviews, and the expectation that your child will return to school. Deregistering removes the option to keep trying and releases your child from all that pressure. You cannot recover from an experience that you are still living.

Parents often see the light in their child's eyes dim when they start school and are attuned to the signs of stress in their child. You see it when your child arrives home deflated, agitated, tired, listless, disconnected and in states of shutdown or meltdown. These are normal responses to highly stressful and intense situations, but should not be a normal occurrence in day-to-day living.

To even begin to recover from a flawed or poor experience, it must be behind you.

Ground zero

With the pressure lifted, what follows is often relief and release.

For some this will be a smooth and gentle time, not that different to taking a holiday or having a long weekend. Some children are less impacted by their schooling and carry on in their merry authentic and autodidactic way. It's not unheard of for some young people to have clear ideas about what they want to do, and once free from school they dive into their current pursuits wholeheartedly. There will still be an adjustment to be made and time getting into a new pace and rhythm of life, but it will come together peacefully.

Alice has two daughters – the eldest remains in secondary school and her youngest was deregistered when she nine years old and has been unschooled for the past two years. She reflected on what happened once they made the decision to remove her from school:

> “First and foremost, it was a massive relief, because that last year at school had been such a struggle. Once we stopped and looked back, we realised that it wasn't just that last year, it was her entire school career.

The sad truth is that we often see children in a state of breakdown before they can move fully into unschooling. For some children, their day-to-day experience of living has been so exhausting and debilitating that they need an extended period of rest and recovery. This can often look like children doing nothing, spending extended periods of time in bed, in their bedroom or curled up on the sofa watching TV. Low moods, little conversation, poor hygiene and small appetite are also common indicators that life has been overwhelming and too much for too long. It often looks like your child has regressed, and you wouldn't be wrong for wondering if you had made the right decision. Things appear to have gotten worse. It can be hard to watch as parents, and it can be difficult not to be tempted into cajoling them to do more than they are able.

Alice described to me what those first few months looked like for her daughter:

> “We were at home a lot. In the early days, she was still recovering. She was quite clearly burnt out. She did a lot of watching programmes. She'd watch the same things over and over, they were her favourite things, her comfort things. She did a lot of watching and we did a lot of talking. I'd go up and join her in a room, or she'd come and look for me, and we'd sit downstairs and just chat about things. Sometimes we'd chat about what she might want to do, and other times we would chat about her programmes.
>
> I think at that point she was doing one activity a week, which was horse riding. That was something she'd started before she left school but had stopped because she just didn't have the capacity by the weekend to be doing anything. That was one of the first things she wanted to bring back in, because the instructor was a safe person. She bonded with the woman who taught it, but that was only one thing a week. The rest of the time we'd spend at home, playing lots of Sylvanian Families® [collectible animal figures].

This doesn't look like school at all. You may be hard pushed to find the learning that is happening (we will get to that part!), but your child needs this stage so that what comes next is built on a foundation that is strong and healthy. Don't panic! Just like Alice, focus on spending time together doing whatever it is that they are doing, watching TV, joining them where they are and doing things they enjoy, like horse riding or playing Sylvanian Families. Essentially, this is what intentionally creating that safe space for your child looks like.

Rebecca talked about her experience when her son left school:

> “When he came out of school, and I think this is probably an assumption for a lot of people if they take their child out of school because they're struggling, they think that they will be fine. If you can just take away some of that pressure, then they'll be fine, because you've reduced it. We found that you had to take all the pressure away. You really had to completely let go, because for a while, we were saying, 'We need to get out every day, we need to go to these groups, it's really important that you get physical exercise all the time'. All those things that you know yourself, that they are good for you in general.
>
> We have had an incredibly difficult journey coming out. We had six months of awful daily meltdowns that we can now see were burnout, and all of the trauma coming out. It's stuff that you think, 'That won't happen to me', and it was really devastating. He just needed to be sort of constantly met where he's at. We said we've just got to stop. Literally just stop and whatever he needs, whatever he wants to do, that's where we're at, and that can be literally lying in bed for weeks on end. It has meant being very limited by him, which has been hard, but has also been the quickest and only way to recovery. So, the process of letting school go has been very traumatic, at times, but also very rich.

Living in a bubble

It's not uncommon to feel like your child's world has become very small during the recovery phase, but there are always things we can do to help support this process. Rebecca's approach to accepting where her son was emotionally and his current ability to engage is just one way in which we can make things better for our children.

Having a consistent, familiar, safe adult (or two) is not to be underestimated. The act of being fully **present, available and attentive** to your child and responsive to their personal and individual needs is a soothing balm. This leads to healing. Focusing on providing a space where your child feels safe, both emotionally and physically, is an active step towards providing them with extended periods of time in which they feel relaxed and comfortable. Your child is instinctively doing what they need to right now; trusting them and supporting them in their recovery process is the first, somewhat gigantic, step into unschooling – meeting them where they are, listening to what they are telling you, and doing it with grace and full acceptance of this moment (see Table 4.1).

Table 4.1. Creating a bubble

Instead of:	Try:
Setting an alarm every morning...	Allowing your child to rest and relax and let them sleep until they naturally wake
Sticking to a set plan for the day...	Centring your child and listening to their voice by being flexible and responding to the moment
Having 'high expectations' for behaviour...	Rebuilding and repairing your relationship by lowering demands and expectations
Worrying about their academics...	Redirecting your energy and spending time researching and learning about unschooling
Encouraging them to do something else (get out of bed/go for a walk/stop screaming)...	Meeting them where they are with grace and kindness – remember that they are doing the best they can

While your child is in this recovery phase, you could take the time to gather information about unschooling. The parents I interviewed all talked about books they had read and podcasts they had listened to that supported them, gave them comfort and reassurance, and deepened their knowledge about unschooling. You can find a full and comprehensive list at the end of this book for your further reading.

Restore: expanding the bubble

At some point children will begin to emerge from the state of recovery, some more tentatively than others. The process isn't a step-by-step programme whereby they smoothly move from one state to the next, though. It's more like a cha-cha-cha – two steps forward and one step back.

Remember that it may only be a brief moment or a few hours that your child seems more engaged or more joyful or does something new. This is because your child is tentatively trying out what happens if they ask a question, step outside the front door or share an opinion. They are testing the water from their established point of safety, and discovering what happens if they want to go out and what happens when they have had enough and want to come home (for example). This means that you will primarily be continuing to focus on what strengthens your relationship and listening to your child and practising your nonchalant mode: no fanfares, no big celebration, no comment on them finally wanting to do something or being in a better mood. Keep it nice and easy.

Rebecca recalls a moment when she observed a shift in her child from burnout:

> " What I've seen is how school took away their ability to know their own body in a very short space of time. For months he would just shout, 'Mum, water'. Children are immobilised by the school environment and they lose the ability to state clearly and confidently what they need. It took months for that to come back, and slowly now he moves when he needs to, asks for things politely. The language, self-reflection and bodily autonomy return.

Alice expanded on her daughter's Sylvanian Families play once she had been out of school a few months:

> " Sylvanian Families was a big, big interest for her. I think the amount of time she spent playing that demonstrated, for me, how much she still needed that role-play and that free play stuff that you can't do in school because you grow, past the age of four, so you're not allowed to do that anymore.
>
> She'd obviously needed to carry that on for much longer. But also, she was so strung out from school that she wasn't even playing much

> at home, and suddenly, without school, she was. We were delving into scenarios and talking about stuff and getting engaged in play at such a deeper level than she'd ever done before. Having the time and space to do it and the energy to do it made that possible.

This is the bit where you can reset your child's experience. They now get a say in how their time is spent. They can change the course of the game they are playing or activity they are doing. They can start and finish it when they are ready to. They can stay as long or as little as they like in one place. They can have ready access to food/drink/ their favourite teddy/sensory regulation tools.

It is like when we go to a museum. In our early days when my children were young, we went with no planned agenda; occasionally we would have arranged to meet another family there, but not always. We would wander around the museum at will. We moved from one display or room to another as our feet took us or as we were invited to by interesting displays. Sometimes we only made it to the play areas! We arrived at a time that suited us, stayed as long or as little as we liked and then headed home. As the children became older, we would return to the same museums, sometimes because we knew that the play area had the best zip line, or because they wanted to see something specific, like the obsidian on display, and we would go with the purpose to see that one thing but often stay longer and look at other items that caught their attention.

It is an entirely different approach to exploring a museum than a school trip. School trips are meticulously planned. The worksheet is there to make sure your child looks at the displays and items that someone else has deemed important for them at this time. They can only spend the allotted time in each section. They definitely can't leave when they are finished or tired, and they might get 5 minutes on the play area if they finish their lunch in time. Can you see the difference? Table 4.2 outlines some of the differences between visiting a museum on a school trip and as an unschooling family day out.

Table 4.2. Not a school trip

The school museum trip	The unschool museum day out
The teacher specifies the purpose for the visit	Time to explore the things your child wants to see and discover more about
Focus on the information needed for the worksheet	Your child is able to ask the questions they would like answers to and gather the information that interests them
Must arrive, walk around and leave according to the schedule	You and your child are able to arrive when works for you, walk around at your own pace and leave when you are ready to
Get to play on the play area for 5 minutes when you have finished your lunch, if you're lucky	Your child can play in the play area all day if you want to
One-off trip	You and your child can return as many times as you like

A few of their favourite things

It's a shocking truth that many parents have been told that to make school more appealing they should make their home uncomfortable and unpleasant. Now you are going to **make your home a nest**, as comfortable and as cosy as possible. In the same way that animals prepare for winter hibernation, gather everything that your child needs to feel warm and snug and safe, cared for and thought about.

Many children aren't ready to leave their bedroom let alone the house. It's okay to provide them with low lighting, quiet surroundings, their favourite playlist on repeat and food in bed, and for them to wear pyjamas when they do emerge. Healing doesn't have to be about leaving the house; it can be leaving the bedroom.

Create a home where the things they love are as available and as easy to access as possible. Boxes of LEGO, the games console set up, craft items in easy reach, an exercise ball in the room, an instrument to hand, books lying around, their favourite blanket within reach. Think about the things your child enjoys and have those things available. They only need to be there, ready, like part of the furniture. A silent invitation, not an expectation. An opportunity offered peacefully so that your child is able to engage when they are ready, and they feel able to rather than in response to any pressure or expectation from those around them.

During this period of time, when a child is beginning to leave school-type ideas behind them, it is often difficult to know what to fill your days with. It can be useful to approach this time as if it was a holiday. Consider what your child would like to do, what local attractions or places of interest they might like to visit, what activities they would like to try, what local social meet-ups they could look into, and schedule in lots of time to rest. **Allow for unstructured and unplanned periods of time.** This is an important and useful tool for unschooling families wherever you are on your journey. Start now with the intention of there being a period of time where your child isn't required to do anything for anyone other than themselves.

A FEW OF THEIR FAVOURITE THINGS

Take some time to compile a list of your child's favourite things. Anything from toys, games, people, or places, to a den under the table, a book/film/show they watch and rewatch. Anything that they enjoy, anything that they use to regulate themselves, anything that lights them up or brings them a sense of peace.

It can be a delicate time, emerging from recovery and stepping into something new, a new way of living and learning. It will very much depend on your child's personal experience, and their personality. It will need you to be attuned to your own child and responsive to what they need and how they are feeling. There is no rush. Keep unschooling values in mind as you reset your family's approach to life and learning, and let those values influence the small decisions you are making, one at a time. **Apply your values to each moment.**

Recreate: great big bubbly bubbles

Once your child has taken time to recover from their schooling and you have begun to re-establish emotional safety and values within your home, stepping into a new way of learning will be smoother. It can be an exciting time for you as the parents to witness your child engaging in the world again, stepping out beyond their safety bubble that they had created for themselves. As unschooling parents, we want to join them on their waves of enthusiasm and joy.

What I hope you will see from your child are steps beyond doing things that are safe for them. That they will begin to look outward a little (or a lot) and see the world with awe and wonder. That their natural curiosity, which has previously been trampled on, will begin to return and that they will begin to be excited, or simply at peace, about what they are doing.

Things you might witness in your child might include simply laughing or smiling when they are doing something. It doesn't matter what it is – gaming, reading a book, looking out of the window, playing with friends. There will be a sense that they are comfortable, relaxed and having a good time. That spark that so many parents tell me goes out when they go to school is returning.

Another way you will notice your child is stepping into their own natural growth and development is that they begin to ask questions. It might be invisible at first. They might ask them in their own head. You might observe daydreaming, or a new sense of wonder at things (great or small), gasps of amazement at something they see on the TV or at the local swimming pool, them pausing to play with the water running from the tap or pondering the different handles on their dresser and wardrobe. It might be that they ask a question out loud.

Their own sense of awe and wonder is returning. The things they notice that they find interesting, that they are drawn to from within their selves. It might be that you see them returning to the same thing repeatedly and their sustained interest in a game or activity is growing. It could be that they invite you in, want you to come and watch what they are doing, or show you something they have noticed (in our house this often happens with the clouds, stars, sunsets and moon). They are asking you to witness what they are doing and how they see the world, and to share in it with them.

It can be tempting to jump on any sign that your child is ready to do something or 'learn'. 'Go to' ways of supporting learning often reflect our schooled ideas and experiences. As we seek to unschool and do something in line with our child's natural self, it is important to respond in gentle and slower ways because we are aiming to find ways that suit them. Check out Table 4.3 for some practical ideas to use as well as ones to avoid at this stage.

Table 4.3. Practical ideas for recreating a life of learning

Experiment with responding in the following ways:	Avoid suggesting the following ideas:
Simply answer their questions with the answer they asked for Notice the things and activities they enjoy Make more time available for them to do the things they enjoy Have resources readily available for the things they are doing Create space or increasing space in your home for them to enjoy the things they love doing Invest in one new item at a time	Introducing a curriculum Setting up a project Making a lapbook Suggesting they write a diary of their learning Signing up to a class Finding a tutor Investing heavily in resources or equipment

When the bubble bursts

This whole process can often feel very delicate. While there are things you can do to enable recovery and step into restoration, there will also be times when you discover something that doesn't work. Remember you are all doing a new thing and learning together. Go gentle with yourself, as well as with your child.

Nicola shared how her and her children tried things out, made mistakes, and ultimately found what worked well for her children:

> "There was a home educating group that was once a month that I tried to take them to a few times. That was just a total disaster. My

son would always lose his shit completely, and it was always absolutely horrific. I think I lasted about four months and then never took him again, because it was just way too difficult for all of us.

We basically couldn't go to other groups. I wouldn't say we were particularly isolated; we just took refuge. We did what worked and didn't do what didn't work. And the world got much, much, much smaller for both my children for a while.

From school to unschool

Within a year of deregistering from school, most family members should feel more relaxed. There will be contributing factors that are different for each family, including finances, school experiences, family dynamics, number and age of your children. In my experience, the younger the child or the less time they have had in school, the quicker and more straightforward this process is.

There will certainly be more moments that are lighter and calmer. There will be more days where you will be able to see the positive impact it is already having on your child's life and learning. There will be days when you don't even worry about what you are doing or what your child is doing, and you will be getting on with the business of living your life together.

Rebecca made this clear as she was talking with me:

> “Even with all of that we've been through in the last two years, there's not a single bit of me that's like, ‘Oh God, we shouldn't have done that’. There's not, you couldn't find a speck within me. Despite the trauma. We're two years in since leaving school, and now they're craving things.

At some point, beyond the delicate nature of the bubble or the tentative steps of emerging, there will come increasing moments of ease and joy. Your child will take a step (or two) into the world (or your own garden, kitchen or TV room) and ask a question out loud, or pick up a toy and play the way they want to, or choose with abandonment the show they want to watch.

Your child will still need you right alongside them, to provide them with the support they need, the thing that makes it possible for them to do this activity. Keeping your child central to this process is key. Meeting them where they are, observing and supporting them, responding to their needs and allowing them to emerge when they are ready, and in ways that they are ready, is what makes this all possible for your child.

Recovering from school and dismantling all our schooled thoughts often takes a lifetime (not a year!). There is a steep learning curve and rapid adjustment that takes place in the first few months. This leads to the beautiful restoration of relationships with themselves and one another. Not forgetting the renewal of relationships with the wider community and the world. This is healing.

Principles to live by

- The process is important.
- Be present, available and attentive.
- Make your home a nest.
- Allow for unstructured and unplanned periods of time.
- Apply your values to each moment.

Chapter 5

Learning Without a Curriculum

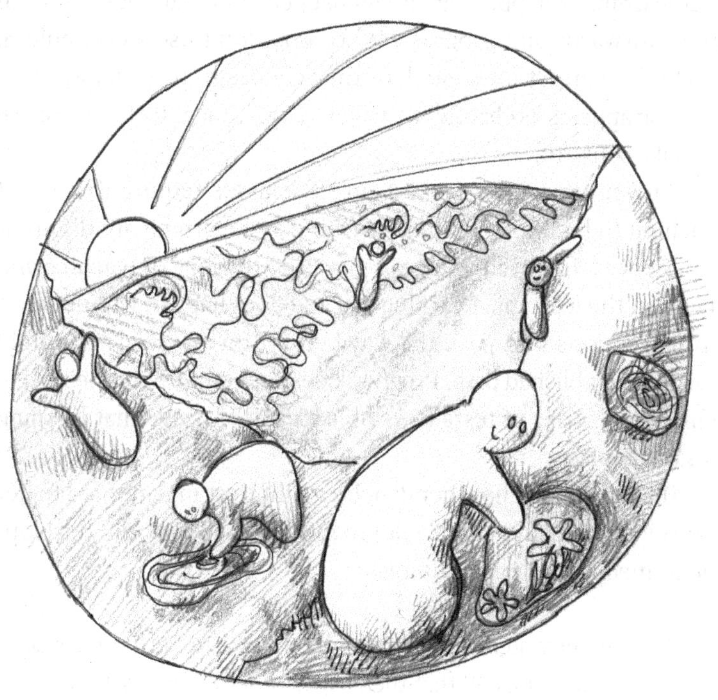

Knowing that learning happens without a curriculum is one of the hallmarks of unschooling. Understanding that **learning happens all the time**, wherever and whatever your child is doing, is a central idea in the unschooling philosophy. It is often the starting place for many families – removing curriculums, workbooks, tutors and teaching from your day to day. However, the absence of these school-like methods can leave you wondering what you are going to do. Removing these elements can leave a void. If you don't have a curriculum that tells you what to do, how will your child know what to do? If you don't have a list that says what they should learn and how old they should be when they learn it, then how will you know that they are on the right track? If you don't have a predefined timetable to follow, how do you know how long to spend on things? And how do you make sure that there are no gaps in their learning?

It can be difficult to let go of curriculums, classes, worksheets and tutors. They are familiar and give you some concrete assurance that learning is happening, or will happen, and that your child will move forwards and progress. When you don't use a curriculum, or children aren't interested, or they choose to play all day, their learning appears as chaotic as their activity is, and it feels impossible to make sense of.

Curriculums, courses and (most) classes require the use of teaching to be implemented. Teaching and learning are different experiences. In unschooling we put aside the idea of teaching and focus on the learning. Learning can and does happen without a set of instructions that pave the way before you and lead your child down an established path. Progress does happen without their being a plan or a series of tests to establish gaps or prove that learning has taken place.

Alice explained how her daughter's interest in dance led to her improving her physical development, musicality, social development, media studies and literacy:

> “My daughter's interest in dance meant that she found the initial experience rewarding and that then led to other things. Taylor is dancing plenty, and you can see her physically, more confident, so much stronger, more graceful, more coordinated, just because she's doing these dance classes. She's working with people, she's entered a choreography competition at the Dance School, and she's agreed to work in a group. She gave me a couple of names of people who spoke to her

> and they've made a little group of four. They came round yesterday for the first time. She doesn't really know them. They know each other, but they've not really spoken. They spent two-and-a-half hours out in the garden working on this routine, videoing it, giving each other feedback. This is amazing. This is not something I would have pictured her doing ever, and it's just lovely. It turned out that one of the girls really loves Sylvanians, so they went and did a bit of that as well. It's just lovely seeing her move on in her own time, in her own way.

Teaching and learning

Teaching and learning are different things. When a person is teaching anything, they cannot guarantee that the recipient is learning what they are intending them to learn, although there are many ways of increasing the chances that specific aims are achieved. This is where we get the idea from that learning must be explicitly talked about or identified through written aims. It also relies heavily on rewards and consequences for non-compliance and providing external motivation. These are techniques that are required by those who are teaching to increase the chances that their points are being learned.

In reality, learning is not the same as teaching. Learning is unique to the learner. Learning is everywhere and the world is full of curiosities and wonders if your child is provided with the time to engage with them, and if their internal motivation is nurtured through validation and facilitation. Shifting your gaze from considering what your child is being taught, or what you think they should be taught, and observing what they are learning and then moving to trusting that whatever they are doing they are learning, will enhance your child's unschooling experience.

The ladder of learning

Your child hasn't read the child development handbook. They don't know that they are being measured and monitored and expected to develop their skills in the same order and time frame as every other child on the planet. They don't know that they should be following a step-by-step programme – for example, standardising the idea that young children roll over, sit up, crawl, walk and then run, and setting learning out like a ladder that is to be climbed one rung at a time. At the bottom of the ladder the knowledge or skill is simple and rudimentary. As you climb the ladder, the new skill or knowledge gained is a degree more sophisticated than the one before.

This model is used in the National Curriculum and in most other school curriculums too, in the UK and around the world. At the top of the ladder, the completion of the curriculum is the pinnacle of knowledge, skills and understanding in the given subject. Content is set out as linear – there is an end goal, and children work on achieving the next step up the ladder to reach it. When you get stuck part way up, you spend time figuring out the next part before you master it and can move further on up. There are no jumping sections or going sideways; you have to keep moving upwards to complete that course and succeed.

Unfortunately, children don't know that they should learn to crawl before they can walk (some children get straight to walking), they don't know that they should learn their phonetic alphabet before they can read whole words (some children don't do either). They also don't know that they aren't allowed to forget what they have learned or spend enormous amounts of time doing the new thing repeatedly. They don't know that they aren't allowed to get bored of what comes next in one subject and be distracted by some other curiosity that catches their attention. They don't know that, until that is, they go to school and find out that what they want to do is unimportant, that their own questions and interests are irrelevant, and that if they don't fit the mythical unicorn of normal, they are, in fact, wrong.

The carrot and the stick

For this model to work, there is a system to keep children on the ladder and moving upwards. Rewards are used to encourage children in the right direction: stickers, 'well done' stamps, certificates and a class teddy bear to hold. Merit systems, extra privileges and day trips out. Punishments are used to deter a child from not complying:

staying in at playtime, sitting on their own, red cards and sad faces, writing lines, detention and exclusion.

These are all examples of external motivation. Things that encourage your child to learn the required things by giving them a reward for achieving the set goal or a punishment when they are distracted, disinterested or unable to achieve the set outcome. This changes how a child views themselves, how they view what is important, and the reasons why they choose to engage in an activity. The external reward becomes valuable and their internal motivation becomes diminished, insubstantial and lost.

Embracing the diversity of learning timelines

In reality learning and development are much more asynchronistic, unpredictable and individualised. Even when a child progresses well and sequentially in one of the established areas of learning, they are unlikely to do so in each of them. It is a ridiculous notion, once you have known more than one child, to measure all children against a perfect version of typical. It doesn't exist. A great harm is done by constantly comparing a child to this mythical standard, spending concentrated amounts of time focusing on how a child falls short and requiring them to participate in exercises and extra tuition to assist them in achieving their (perceived) lacking skills or knowledge, as outlined by another person's artificial standard.

School children are measured, tested and found wanting week in, week out throughout their school years. They are graded, scored, represented via different data graphs and bell charts. They are discussed vigorously in staff meetings – especially in the case of children who find themselves continuously at the end of the bell curve. This is micro-monitoring. It is an invasive, degrading and miserable experience. It is also unnecessary.

Tests are sold to us on the pretence that they aid learning (the weekly spelling test, for example) or that they help teachers and other educational professionals track teaching and learning (end of topic assessments or end of year exams, for example). And arguably, within the mainstream education system this may be the simplest way of acquiring all that information. At home, it is wholly possible to live a life without the need to test in order to know that progress has occurred.

The web of learning

Children who don't go to school are free to jump off this linear ladder of learning (or to never even put a foot on it). They don't need a curriculum to tell them what to learn and when. They get to decide. If your child gets up in the morning and wants to bake cakes without using a recipe, then that's what they do. If they want to count how many cartwheels they can do across the garden, they can do that. If they want to watch the same film they watched yesterday, and the day before, they can do that too. If they want to connect online with a friend and spend three hours trying to defeat the Ender Dragon in *Minecraft*, then go for it.

Learning comes from actively choosing what they are doing, following their own curiosities and questions, and making connections across all of life. Instead of developing skills and knowledge according to someone else's preset curriculum, a separate ladder for each topic or subject, learning looks more like a web of connected ideas drawn from their own life experiences. **Learning is connecting ideas together.** They join together the parts of life that engage them, develop their own knowledge and understanding of the world, and build an ever-changing, developing, shifting, growing web of learning.

This world is not divided into subjects. As your child makes meaningful connections that are based on experiences, conversations, interests, joy, challenges and life, they are building an interconnected understanding of the world. History, geography, science, art and literature all become intertwined in interests in face painting, questions about the pets you keep, playing computer games, films you watch, places you go, skateboarding parks you visit and toys they play with. Conversations in car journeys can seemingly leap from a film that a younger member of the family enjoys to the actors who are in them, to other films they have been in over the decades, and end up on Californian beaches, weather fronts and the political nature of different countries. It might seem nonsensical, but this is how natural learning and connection between all things happens. It is not set out neatly in topics or half-termly plans. It can be bitesize or a deep dive. It can appear to leapfrog from one thing to another to the untrained eye. There can be 'A-ha' moments that are obvious and explicit and loud, there can be extended periods of time where it is difficult to see the learning taking place, there can be intense periods where interests go down rabbit holes for weeks on end, or they keep popping up over the years.

Natural learning is like this. It is non-linear. **Learning pathways are individual and unique.** They circle back round on themselves as your child adds new information and skills to existing information and skills. They make sense of the world by connecting new things to old things and they solidify their existing understanding by re-enforcing the connections they have previously made.

Learning pathways are driven by your child's internal motivation and natural curiosity and developed through rich and meaningful experiences. You can see some examples of how learning can build and develop in Figures 5.1a and 5.1b.

How children learn without a curriculum

Unschooling fosters your child's internal motivation. It reignites and fans the flames of your child's natural curiosity. Your child's ability to learn is like their ability to breathe or their heart beating: it happens all by itself. As an unschooling parent, it is your role to create the conditions in which that can happen freely, and for it to become stronger if it has been lost in their schooling experience.

Schools are experts at using external motivation. This overuse of rewards and consequences reduces internal motivation, which can be seen when children engage better when they know that there is extra playtime at the end of a task or they do their homework only so that they can avoid detention. It can be seen when they don't want to do something unless there is something in it for them (external motivation). Equally it is evident when they are unable to make a decision about what it is that they would like to do, and need someone else to decide for them or affirm their choice.

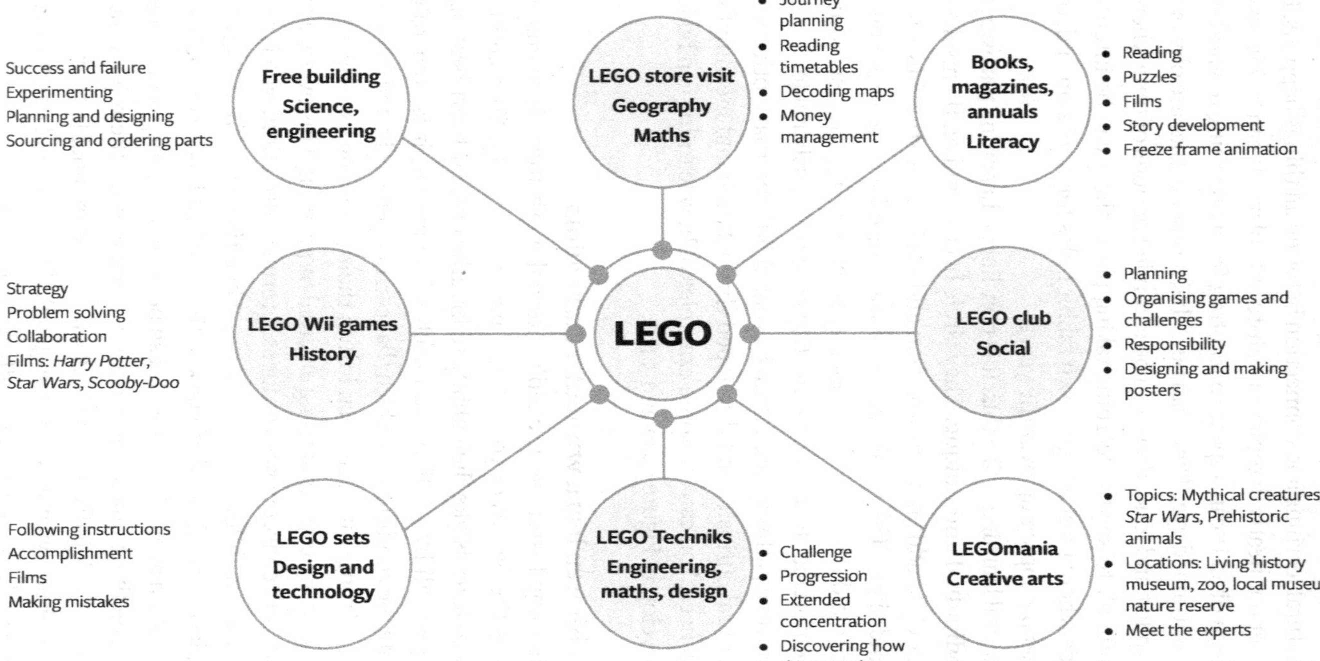

Figure 5.1a. Connected learning: LEGO® mindmap

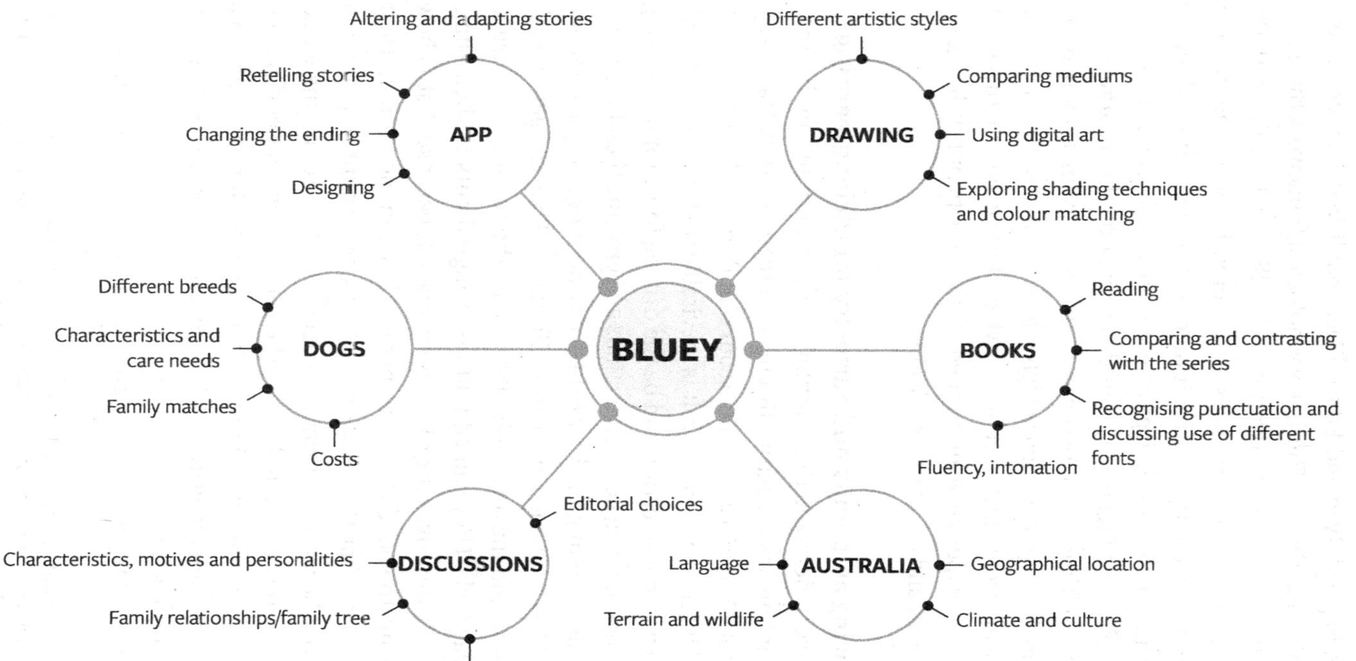

Figure 5.1b. *Connected learning: Bluey learning journey*

In 2015 Richard Ryan and Edward Deci published a paper on self-determination theory.[1] This is a psychological framework that seeks to understand human motivation and wellbeing. It begins with the understanding that individuals are inherently motivated to grow, learn and fulfil their potential. It then sets out how this is done via three fundamental psychological needs: autonomy, competence and relatedness (see Figure 5.4). Self-determination theory argues that when these three basic psychological needs are met, individuals are more likely to experience higher levels of motivation, personal growth and wellbeing. In contrast, when these needs are thwarted, people may experience diminished motivation, poor psychological adjustment and decreased wellbeing.

Nurturing autonomy and curiosity for lifelong learning

When we understand that learning is everywhere and all the time, and that humans are naturally curious creatures, then learning is inevitable. When we respond to our child's natural curiosity with joy and interest and nurture, it is inevitable that that curiosity will remain without question and be the driving force for discovering new things, making new connections and growing their knowledge and understanding of the world. They no longer need someone to say 'This is science' or 'This is life skills'. They can get on with designing and making their sibling a birthday cake as a normal everyday task. They can add different ingredients to their slime to see if it improves it or how it changes it, because that is how they want to spend their afternoon. They can measure up their bedroom so that they can order the right amount of paint and wallpaper because they want to decorate their room this weekend. And you can sit and watch the routine they are performing on the trampoline and share in their joy that they can now do a tuck jump/somersault/remember three moves in a row that they couldn't do before.

Instead of testing, including asking questions for the purpose of

1 Ryan, Richard M. and Deci, Edward L. (2000) 'Self-determination theory and the facilitation of intrinsic motivation, social development, and well-being.' *American Psychologist* 55, 1, 68–78. doi: 10.1037110003-066X.55.1.68.

testing or finding out if they know something, we enlist the skills we have been using since your child arrived. We observe, we witness and we know. Sometimes observing can be intentional. It can help, especially in the early days, to deliberately practise the skill of observing – it is a particularly useful technique when you have a wobble about something. To observe is to see, truly see, what is going on beneath the surface of what may appear mundane or an everyday occurrence.

To witness your child is to share in their joy. It is likely that in asking you to 'Watch me!' your child is seeking to connect with you, acknowledging that you are the one they want to share this with. There is often also a sense of 'I can do this thing'. It might be mixing paint to make new colours, or jumping on to the sofa cushions, or mixing jelly cubes really fast to make a whirlpool. To witness is to acknowledge that this new thing is exciting and wonderous.

Your child will often have 'A-ha' moments. It's a tangible point in time when the penny drops and a new connection is made. One idea joins to another in a concrete moment that is identifiable, commonly with an exclamation of, 'Oh, I have just realised!' or 'Does that mean X is like Y?' or 'I get it now'. To know that your child is progressing and learning (without testing) can be like the 'A-ha' moment that your child has. It is a moment when you realise that they can do this thing or that they know something they didn't know last week/month/year. You don't need a test to prove it; you know it because they are your child and you are actively involved in their life. For you to know your child is for you to have built, or be building, a relationship with them that is as strong and tangible as the natural learning connections they are making.

Cultivating growth through competence

As a preschooler, my eldest was a dream. He was chatty, he loved going to the toddler groups and he engaged in the activities. He could do a whole range of things that his peers were also doing: climbing, using scissors for craft, chatting with others, listening to stories – he would have scored quite well on the developmental assessments. But he couldn't do everything. One of the things that bothered me, and I don't know why it did, was that he didn't know his colours. He couldn't tell me which flower was red, or pass the yellow paint to his friend, or ask for his favourite green t-shirt. I made a conscious effort to point out coloured things to him and I was frustrated by his inability to 'get it'. This is surely basic preschool stuff. Many nursery settings create entire topics based on colours – for example, The seasons, Famous artists, *The Very Hungry Caterpillar*. Preschool books are full of colour editions, such as *Maisy's Colours*, *Spot's Colours* and stories about rainbows. It is developmentally appropriate, according to those who tell us so, for preschool children to know their colours. Not my son.

I don't remember my concern continuing for that long. I settled myself with all the things I knew to be true. Things like, 'He has learned all these other things already', 'He will learn them when he is able to and has a need to', 'He is surrounded by opportunity to learn his colours'. And so, after a short period of time, I took a step away from actively interjecting his life with artificial learning moments and went back to enjoying whatever it was that we were doing together.

You'll be pleased to know that he did learn his colours when he was ready to. He was about six or seven years old when I realised that he knew them. Now, over a decade later and you would never know and, most importantly, he carries no shame about not knowing at the designated time. **Learning happens when we are ready, willing and able.**

I know two children who learned to walk – one when they were 10 months old and the other who mastered it at 30 months old (that's 2½ years). Both these children are adults now and no one would know which was which. Then there are those who don't learn to walk. Children, young people and adults who require assistance, equipment or accommodations to help them move from one place to another. How different their stories might be if their reality was accepted and catered for, if they were seen as competent, instead of making them feel like a burden or always being asked to improve and reach the next target.

Some children enter school being able to read, others already know their alphabet, some can recite their favourite books, and some have no interest in the written word. (In Chapter 8 you can read about how and when unschooled children learn to read, and how they break the mould entirely.) Letting go of those timelines and milestones enables our children to grow in full confidence of themselves and their own abilities.

May Ling described it like this:

> “One has to develop the trust, right? And to develop trust you really need to pay attention. The more you pay attention, the more you'll find evidence that they are trustworthy, that you can trust that your child is learning what's useful for them. Then the more you can do that, the more you'll have ideas of cool things they might be interested in, or something really tangential might pop in and you suggest it, and they run with it. I mean, they might also just say 'no'. The more they don't have expectations of how they should be behaving or how they should be developing, the more they're free to develop and learn, but the moment you start giving them ideas that by now you should be here, the more you make them feel incompetent. People who feel incompetent don't learn very well. They start to retract and start to shrink.

There is an assumption that there is a gold standard for children's development. That children who score highly and 'can do' are in fact doing okay and all is well. That children who can't do certain things at a certain age are struggling in some way (especially if it is literacy, numeracy or social skills). This is the assumption. And within schools, it is often the reality. The school system creates a culture where children unnecessarily experience failure, struggle, shame and disappointment. The reality is that where your child is, is exactly where they are supposed to be (see Figure 5.2).

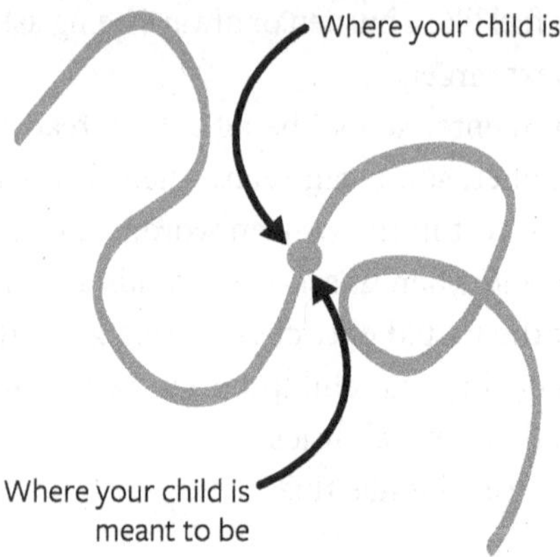

***Figure 5.2.** Where your child is meant to be*

Cultivating growth through connected relationships

When we know that humans grow and learn organically, then logically, progress is inevitable. Whether that progress happens in tiny micro steps, is sequential or occurs in a massive absorption of new skills and knowledge, it doesn't matter. Your child has the innate ability to learn and grow, which means that progress happens.

You will see it when your child brings you a picture they have drawn that shows perspective lines on it to show objects in the distance, and they have recorded a YouTube short to show others. You will see it when they no longer ask you to read the daily challenges on their favourite computer game, when they order something from a menu in an Italian restaurant, when they fix the Wi-Fi. You will see it when they learn to ride a bike and then get better at those skills riding dirt tracks, going faster down hills, persevering up hill, pulling wheelies, riding without holding the handle bars or learning the rules of the road so that they can ride safely.

Sally explained how she witnesses her children's learning:

> “Their learning comes from, essentially, the things they've decided to do, and getting involved in all the things they want to talk about. I see them learning mostly through conversation, conversation is a huge part of our lives. It might be them explaining something to me that they're doing, or just sharing it with me, or sharing videos with me, or

> they tell me about things. Or it might be them asking actual questions about things. These days, the only one there who asks questions is my 12-year-old. My others never ask me anymore; they know more than I do. Often, I'm not aware of what they're learning until they've already picked up quite a lot of information and they're talking through what they're doing.
>
> Some of the learning is very visible. They might have decided they want to join a group, or do something online, or they want to practise languages, or they're looking at videos. They might decide that they want to see a particular documentary on television about something. Some of the learning I can see and it is very, very visible, and some just sort of ticks on in the background, and it comes out through conversation. They're a lot older now, but that's barely changed. That's pretty much how they've done it since the get-go.

When you are with your child and actively involved in their life, you will be able to actively observe and witness things that they now do with less help than before, on their own, or are now supporting others with. You won't be able to not notice how your child is growing and changing all the time. It is reminiscent of when they were little and it seems, suddenly, they are able to roll over and make it from one side of the room to the other, or when they can pick things up and put them straight into their mouth. And always remember that just because they did it once on their own doesn't mean that they will always do it from this moment onwards.

Learning isn't linear. There is ebb and flow. Two steps forward and one step back. It might not happen at a steady pace either. There may be days or weeks where there is very little observable progress, and then a moment where all these new ideas, skills and knowledge make themselves known, like an explosion of new learning. All the while, you will see those moments when the penny drops, or a new skill is better than it was before or fully mastered, because you are your child's partner, present and connected, and you will witness their ongoing learning and development. Figure 5.3 illustrates some of the ways in which learning pathways happen.

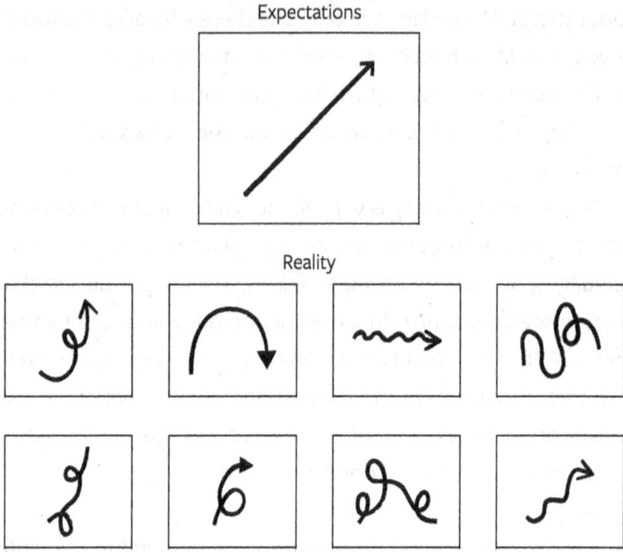

Figure 5.3. Learning journeys

Now, I'm not going to lie – this can become tricker to observe quite as closely when they get older and attend groups without you, or when they spend time working on projects by themselves, or more time in the company of their peers. However, practising the ongoing principles of relationship first, and based on the back of the foundations that have been built over the years (or working on establishing those foundations from this point) does put you in good stead. It builds a foundation for open and honest conversations about the things that are happening in their lives, if you need to know or when they want to share.

The answer to the question whether a child is developing as they should is whole-heartedly 'yes' when we begin to realise that they have the tools within themselves to learn, grow and develop at their own pace and in their own way – when we take a step away from measuring and assessing our child against a mythical typical child and turn our gaze to the child we have, fully accepting where they are at, what they can do and supporting them with the things they need help with until they no longer need that support.

The exercise in Figure 5.4 guides you through how to look at what your child is doing using the model of self-determination theory.

- Increasing opportunities to make meaningful choices
- Having choices valued and facilitated
- Adding credibility to those choices by investing time, effort and space

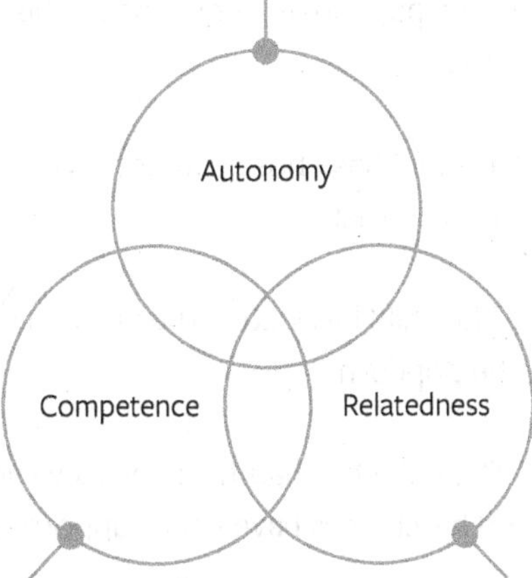

- Home in on the things your child can do
- Provide what they need in order to achieve a task
- Achieve mastery by repeatedly doing the same thing until they are ready to move on
- Allowing your child to try new things and experience challenge when they are ready
- Celebrating with your child and sharing their joy in recognition of their successes

- Foster meaningful relationships
- Feel connected to others
- Have a sense of belonging
- To be accepted, supported, understood and valued
- Feeling safe and supported when with other people

***Figure 5.4.** Heading for the sweet spot*

SELF-DETERMINATION THEORY IN ACTION

Grab a pen and paper and write out a real-life scenario. Think about something that has happened recently that your child has done. You could use the self-determination prompts here – **autonomy, competence, relatedness** – to frame your writing, or after you have written the scenario out you could choose a different highlighter colour for each aspect and highlight where you see them being described in your writing.

Here are some examples:

This is Lloyd. He is five years old. Today Lloyd wants to watch his favourite film and eat popcorn. He has watched this film every day for the last four months, sometimes twice a day. We sit down and watch the film with popcorn in our hands and his siblings colouring and playing LEGO nearby.

Autonomy: The child has chosen what he wants to do and time has been made to do that.

Competence: The child has loaded the film and has been involved in preparing the popcorn.

Relatedness: The child has had his choices valued, his voice has been heard and his choices have been supported.

This is Alfie. He is 10 years old. Today Alfie wants to go to his friend's house for a sleepover for the first time. He has been talking about the idea for a few months and previously arranged dates and then changed his mind. This time he is packed and ready to go. He has his favourite pyjamas, his wash bag and his favourite toy packed. He has made plans with his friend and knows what time they are going to sleep, and they have shared their bedtime routines with each other so they know that they are a good fit. All the parents involved are ready for middle-of-the-night phone calls and for Alfie's parents to come and bring him home if they need to. Alfie knows that he can call at any time and his parents will come and collect him.

Autonomy: Alfie has been fully involved in the planning process and supported by his parents through the long process of attempting previous sleepovers. He has been able to talk through his ideas with all the involved parties, who have worked hard to make them possible.

Competence: The child has taken micro steps and organised things for success – knowing the other family really well, the bedtime routine and how it is going to happen, that he has the tools and ability to call home or confidently speak to his friend's parents.

Relatedness: Being sure the child is comfortable in the other house and with the other family, knowing that he feels safe and relaxed with the people he is staying with, that he can contact his own parents at any time.

This is Angie. She is 12 years old. Today Angie wants to make a giraffe head from a craft kit that she has. She is feeling tired from a busy day yesterday; she woke up after 10am and stays in bed when she wakes up. Her breakfast is brought to her, and she is set up with her laptop. She plays *Minecraft* on her own for a while and continues building on a realm that she has created with her best friend. By lunchtime, she is still in bed. She is reminded about the giraffe head craft kit that she said she wanted to do, but she says that it will be too hard and she doesn't know how to do it. Angie and mum look at it together and after mum has read the instructions, she explains them to Angie. She is really resistant now and repeats that it is too hard and she doesn't want to do it now. Mum takes an interest in Angie's *Minecraft* world and gets a tour of all the builds and an update on the plans for more. Angie spends the afternoon playing *Roblox* with her friends online. Mid-afternoon she gets out of bed and goes out to her dance class. She goes straight back to bed when she gets home. She writes and colours in her journal, plays a card game with mum, and then listens to an audio book as she goes to sleep.

Autonomy: Having the ability to say what she would like to do and plan her day while also being able to tune into her needs in the moment, change her mind and say 'no' right now.

Competence: Engaging in the building process in *Minecraft*.

Challenging herself with new and more complex builds alongside mastering ones she has done many times before.

Relatedness: Being able to offer support and guidance while listening to, hearing and respecting Angie's thoughts and feelings, which helps to address her spoken concerns and how she could navigate 'not knowing' how to do something while also responding to her rising anxiety and placing the activity that was worrying her aside for now.

A world of possibilities

School curriculums are a tiny portion of what is available to learn in a lifetime. Across the world those curriculums are all different. Each one is a slither of what is open to us and what is possible. None of them are the gold standard of learning and knowledge they claim to be. There is no need for the world to be divided into subject areas, there is no need for there to be explicit learning intentions, there is no need to stay wholly focused on one activity for an hour (or other designated lesson period). Learning is always happening. That's not to say that some learning isn't useful or of interest, but that there is so much more available, and by releasing your child from the need to do as someone else prescribes, you are simultaneously opening up a world of avenues to them. They will learn what is important and meaningful to them.

Or, as May Ling put it when I spoke to her:

> “It's their education, it's not yours. Who cares whether or not you can see what they're learning, if they can see what's interesting to them and they know what they're going to do, thank God for that, that you haven't killed that. In some ways, it's like, wind your neck back in, stop being so untrusting of this miracle of life in front of you and let it get on with its life. The desire to measure the learning is going to get in your way and ruin your relationship, because then you don't see them, you're always quantifying. And you're always quantifying by some scale that's been made up.
>
> Putting that aside, I also think if you're with your child, like, present

> with them and watching, you will see learning. It may not be that they're learning what you think they should be learning, but you will see them making connections. Not always physically, but you can tell that they're absorbing something.

In the end, unschooling isn't about *what* your child is learning. It's about nurturing their ability to, and love of, learning. It's about living a life where they can explore, discover, create, wonder and experiment. Children already know how to learn and are intrinsically motivated to do so. Unschooling taps into that and allows that to thrive. Nurturing this love of learning by building a culture where their ideas are valued and facilitated sets them up for a lifetime of being able to discover things for themselves, being confident that they can learn what they want, when they want. A life where they have meaningful and genuine choices, feel competent in their abilities and are connected to the people around them.

Essentially, it looks like living, as Sally explains:

> “ Life and learning are completely entwined. They're inseparable, and so they learn how they learn. They're picking stuff up just because they're interested in it, and it's part of their lives. At no point does anyone think 'I will learn...' Never, ever, ever, in any day, with the exception of, as they're getting older, they say, 'I'd really like to do that, and that requires me to learn this', and then there's some intentional learning in order for something else to happen. That's the only time; otherwise, it all just looks just like living.

Principles to live by

- Learning happens all the time.
- Learning is connecting ideas together.
- Learning pathways are individual and unique.
- Learning happens when we are ready, willing and able.

Chapter 6

How Not to Be a Teacher

We have all had experience of teachers, and some of us have even been teachers. We all know what the job is and what it entails enough to know what teaching a child looks like. Children all over the globe know how to play 'schools', even unschooled children. Who hasn't lined up their teddy bears and dolls in rows sat on the floor before them and then stood up to deliver today's lesson? Once upon a time our parents used to buy us blackboards to write on (usually maths sums, if I remember correctly); nowadays it's a whiteboard and markers so that we can play 'schools' at home. The role of the teacher is to take the knowledge they have and to impart it (teach it) to their pupils, the keen and attentive empty vessels before them. One of the problems with this approach is that children are not passive teddy bears.

Parents often put a lot of preparation or research into home educating when they first set out. Families frequently set up specific learning areas, order in resources and workbooks, maybe sign up to tutors or online programmes. It is a serious undertaking that parents approach with vast amounts of consideration. Caring for our children is just what we do. When it comes to their education, we take what we know and do our best to replicate that at home, at least initially.

What families usually discover, some sooner than others, is that replicating school at home can have disastrous consequences. Putting yourself in a position of 'teacher' rather than 'parent' is likely to make being together 24/7 an unpleasant experience for everyone. There are reasons that the education system is set up the way that it is; rightly or wrongly, it is designed to impart large swathes of information to large groups of children at a time, and it is designed to do it in an orderly and measurable fashion. Those things are unnecessary when you are home educating. You don't have a class of 30 children to manage: it's only your own children you need to focus on. You don't need to measure and record the learning in the same way: your personal observations, continued involvement and deep knowing can inform you of their learning and progress where necessary. And as a pedagogy, unschooling argues that you do not need to impart large amounts of predecided information to your child: by creating a life in which learning can flourish, your child can and will learn what they need to when they need to.

When we no longer put ourselves in the position of teacher, we can maintain our parent–child relationship. Better than that, now that we can be actively involved in each other's lives, this relationship can be strong and connected. Instead of viewing children as an empty vessel (which I am sure you don't) you can now fully embrace who they are and work with them, living a life that is filled with interesting things, helping them to achieve the things they want to achieve and do the things that pique their interest and light them up.

We are not our child's teacher – that is not our role in life, and it doesn't have to be for education to be taking place. Nor do we need to outsource that role to other parties. We do, however, need to take on the role of facilitating our child's life and learning. We need to be actively involved in creating a life where our child can learn with abandon, where they can engage effortlessly with the things that get them excited about the world. Your role now is to facilitate their learning, **helping your child do what they want.**

Not teaching

Many parents' first indication that school isn't right for their child is when they notice the spark in their child go out. When a child first enters Reception class, one of two things happen – either they struggle from the off, or they are really excited! Children who approach those first few days with excitement are often driven by the novelty of it all – the new clothes, haircut and shoes, a lunch box, water bottle and book bag. The whole set-up is designed to be inviting. A room full of toys, colourful walls and smiling, engaging adults and lots of other children to play with are all there to entice them in. Let's not forget that those who have been to nursery have had a big build-up to this moment, and even those who have never been to a preschool find it hard to escape the amount of story books and TV programmes aimed at this age group about the excitement of going to school. By the end of the first six weeks, though, most of these children will have lost their excitement about school, the novelty will have worn off, and the realisation that this is how things are going to be now for a very long time will be dawning on them.

There are also children in every Reception class who find the idea and reality of going to school terrifying. No amount of shiny new things, exciting toys, other children or even a sensory quiet space will sell the idea of being separated from their parent for a whole day. They simply don't want to be there. For these children their integration into school will depend on the school and their approach, but by six weeks most of them will have learned to comply and trot into the classroom without much complaint.

There are times during the school day when individual children do light up. A good teacher, and there are many, will notice what activities, games and classes different children thrive or excel in. However, by the end of a full day at school, parents often see their child with little energy left. Depending on the child this can range from low energy to full overwhelm and meltdown. It is a sign that something is not working for their child. And as the school years go on, the lack of play, higher expectations, decreasing physical movement, standardised approach to learning and use of developmentally inappropriate approaches to teaching continue to negatively impact our child's life experience.[1]

The process of teaching largely ignores the things that children enjoy while simultaneously requiring them to participate in things they have little or no interest in or aptitude for. Children who are unschooled play board games, learn Japanese, perfect nail art, and watch sitcoms. They climb trees, paddle, cartwheel, run around in mazes and paint freely. They do so free from the restriction of a timetable or the requirement to stop what they are doing and do something instructed by an adult. They do so without hiding their interests away, and most of them play for years longer than their schooled peers.

They also empty their toys everywhere, use the products in the bathroom to make the biggest bubbles they can, bake without recipes, build dens out of cardboard boxes, and sit and play with their pets. The variety is endless, the possibilities are everywhere, and how they engage with the world is an open book. This is not so with teaching, where there is a set agenda, a set curriculum, a set path. It is a completely different approach.

Unschooled children may occasionally experience boredom, not knowing what they want to do, but they will not retreat into themselves because of lack of options and lack of enthusiasm or

1 Gray, Peter (2011) 'What Einstein, Twain, & forty eight others said about school.' *Psychology Today*, 26 July. www.psychologytoday.com/us/blog/freedom-learn/201107/what-einstein-twain-forty-eight-others-said-about-school

engagement in an activity. They may feel agitated when their current experience doesn't match their expectation, but they don't need to resign themselves to repeating it again next time. They may look at the things their friends are doing, but instead of not being able to join in (because the instructions they have been given by the teacher are different) they can change what they are doing or have a go later. So that spark in their eyes isn't dimmed as it is for so many of their schooled counterparts.

Resisting teachable moments

When we first come across the idea that learning is everywhere and can happen at any time, it is often tempting to harness the more obvious times by turning them into 'teachable moments'. This is another way that we, as the adults, can feel like we are doing something that is educational with our child. It is also a trap! There is a fine line between your child asking a specific question and wanting to be told how to work out the answer or be given more information.

Teachable moments are those times when we turn a simple question, which usually has a simple answer, into an opportunity to impart knowledge or set out to find out more. It is a moment that is presented to us by our child but is then taken over, usually enthusiastically, by the adult. It is a sure way to stamp out any potential further interest and to make them resistant to coming to you to ask questions or share their excitement about other things.

For example, when your child asks what the time is, it feels like a good opportunity to capture the moment and show them how to tell the time. Simply answering the question they asked is usually the best response. In due course there will most likely come an interaction when they become interested in the clock that you use to give them the answer. In due course they may ask how you read the time. In due course you may point out the digital clock on the kitchen oven. They may ask why two clocks in the same room are showing different times. Or why there are two clocks on the sat nav that are showing different times. Or you may show them your analogue watch that has no numbers on it.

Teachable moments also include trying to encourage your child to do things themselves or give things a try – identifying something your child can't do yet, like cutting using scissors, or putting on their socks, or reading a word, and urging them to have a go. These well-meaning attempts are fuelled by the schooled idea of identifying your child's difficulties and focusing on what they can't do. This is not the same as supporting your child in an unschooling context.

Teachable moments are focused on *teaching* your child something, whether that is imparting ideas and knowledge or building a skill. Turning everyday interactions into a mini project or a chance to intentionally teach your child can be appealing, but it is not recommended. A quick rule of thumb is, if a partner or a friend asked you the same thing, what would you do? How would you answer?

Emotional safety and support

In Chapter 2 we talked extensively about the amount of time and effort that parents put into creating an emotionally safe and supportive environment for their children. The importance of putting these foundations in place and sustaining a home and a life where children feel accepted, nurtured and cared for was emphasised.

Sally reminded me of this when we chatted together:

> "My role's really been to be non-judgmental, and always supportive. Be the person that they can bring their thoughts and ideas to. It's not passive. It's holding that space for them, so that they can be thinking and doing and always have someone to bounce that with or ask for help. It's being available.

This is important to mention again, before we talk about some of the practical ways we facilitate our children's learning. We are culturally wired to be busy and be seen to be actively doing things to enable our children's education. Similarly, we can worry when our children choose or need to rest more than makes us comfortable due to their lack of activity and engagement. What I don't want us to forget as we explore the hands-on things that we can do is that emotional safety and support come first and help guide what our practical support looks like.

Facilitating

The question is, if you are not the teacher and you are not using a curriculum, what are you doing and how are you doing it? It is natural to fall back into using techniques that you are familiar with. Table 6.1 provides some alternatives to being the teacher and what facilitating, partnering and dancing could look like.

Table 6.1. Facilitating, partnering and dancing

Instead of being the teacher and:	Try:
Focusing on what they can't do (yet)...	Making things easier for them
Encouraging independence...	Doing things for them or with them
Utilising teachable moments...	Simply answering the questions they have or helping with the task they are asking for help with
Following curriculum suggestions...	Providing a range of resources, opportunities and ideas for them
Being separated by school and work...	Spending lots of time with your child
Using a timetable to plan your child's learning...	Leaning into their questions and curiosities
Automatically saying 'no'...	Saying 'yes' to their ideas and requests
Valuing core subjects (or even curriculum subjects)...	Being interested in what they are doing
Insisting on independence...	Playing with them and joining them in their activities
Using a curriculum to tell you what your child should be learning and when to learn it...	Expanding their interests and passions and showcasing the wider world
Making all the decisions...	Collaborating with all those involved through discussions and working together to generate and implement ideas
Setting targets or goals at the beginning of a year or term...	Discussing how to make things possible as and when your child's ideas present themselves

Unschooling does not happen in isolation. Being 'self-directed' does not mean working by yourself. It has little to do with working independently from the age of five or always knowing what they want to do. If anything, adult involvement is higher when we are home educating, and this is particularly true when we are unschooling. It is true that there is markedly more input from the child into what their day-to-day looks like, but as attentive and involved adults in their lives, we are the ones who support them, from meeting their physical needs (feeding, watering, sleep/rest etc.) to helping them achieve (or at the very least, work towards achieving) their big ideas – we are with them every step of the way.

We become facilitators in our child's life when we are unschooling. In the context of unschooling, to facilitate means to **make things easier for your child.** This means that we make things possible for them in any way that they need us to.

Doing things *for* your child

1. *Making things easier for them to do the thing they want to do.* Removing the barriers they have because they don't yet have the skill: for example, cutting out the shapes they want (or a range of shapes) so they can stick them on paper, or putting clothes in the car so they can get changed there and ease transitions. We want to make learning possible. Beyond that, we want to make it straightforward and remove any arbitrary barriers that we can. This enables them to do more of the things they love and concentrate on the things they are good at. Making things easier for them adds to their joy and ease, their emotional safety, and relaxed happy brains.

   As Rebecca explained:

> “When my daughter comes up with something that she's interested in doing, we just try and work out a way to make that happen. The ideas have to come from them. In our family, there is strong opposition to anything that the adults suggest, and they are sensitive to any real or perceived pressure. Facilitating what they want to do is essential.

2. *Doing things for them*, and doing it with grace and compassion. Make them a plate of food, brush their hair, read a page of a story, tie their shoelaces (actually, I highly recommend getting elastic laces or Velcro). Doing these things even when you know that they can do them themselves. Doing my child's hair becomes a touch point in our day, a moment of connection and shared experience – it is an essential part of the make-up of our relationship. Sometimes children need or ask others to help them because the ritual of it is grounding in their day or because what they are really in need of is a moment of connection. They will do things for themselves soon enough and they will also continue to know how to ask for help.

3. *Creating a life of learning also involves providing physical resources and opportunities for your child.* In the beginning it may be about collecting a variety of resources, toys, games or materials for your home or taking them to different events, museums, galleries, outdoor venues such as forests, beaches and parks, and all the while being responsive to your child. It might mean getting toys out of cupboards and setting them up for them ready, or rotating toys if you have limited space. It could mean subscribing to craft/science/interest boxes, magazines, charities or apps. It might be investing in membership to a local indoor play area (very useful in the winter months), museum, national organisation or local library, and then being able to make good use of those places.

   This doesn't need to be costly. Sourcing second hand toys, visiting charity shops, swapping resources among the home ed community and recognising the versatility in simple things such as sticks and stones and shells are all a good place to start. Providing resources for them means creating physical space where those things can happen freely and uninterrupted, with abundant time for them to be explored.

Partnering
Doing things *with* your child

1. *Spending lots of time with your child and leaning into their questions and curiosities.* Saying 'yes' when they want to stop and watch a snail climb a wall; saying 'yes' when they want to stay home instead of going out; saying 'yes' when your teen wants to talk to you at midnight; saying 'yes' when they want you to sit and colour with them; saying 'yes' when they invite you into their play and leaving when they want to play with their friends on their own; saying 'yes' when they only want to make icing; saying 'yes' when you go to a museum to look at the LEGO exhibition and all they want to do is sit and play with the bricks in the interactive area (and you could have stayed and played with LEGO at home). **Be generous** with your time and energy, where you can.

   Leaning into their questions and curiosities also means considering when you say 'no', taking a pause and seriously questioning whether you can do the thing your child is requesting. All too commonly 'no' is the default answer, but as we move further into being with our child and partnering them, making room to say 'yes' will also mean saying 'no' to other things. It will also mean catching yourself before you automatically say 'no', leading you to examine your reasons why and causing you to reconsider.

   Steve shared how important this revelation was for him as he began to embrace unschooling:

> Something that kind of, like, kicked in early on was this idea of not coming up with an arbitrary 'no'. Once the kids were able to ask for things, 'I can't be bothered to help facilitate that right now' wasn't an acceptable answer.

2. *Simply being interested in what your child is doing* is an easy way to facilitate their learning. Playing their games with them and joining in on their terms is a fantastically good use of your

time. This will change as your child grows, but there is usually room to do activities together, go out together, or simply have a catch-up and a chat about their day. Showing your support in this way affirms and substantiates their choices. In this way they grow and sustain confidence in themselves and in their ability to make choices.

3. *Getting to know your child by being with them means that you can tailor the things you have available.* When your child shows a particular interest or passion in something, offering them options that are linked to or sparked by that interest is one way to work in partnership with them. This expands their opportunities by working in partnership with their flow.

   Sally talked about this when we chatted:

> “When they were younger, it was making sure there were a lot of options for them, even if they didn't want them. It was trying to help them figure out ways that they could expand on interests they had. If they were feeling like they did want more friends, then figuring out what kind of group might be good. So really trying to meet the needs as they would come up.

IDEAS MENU

The world is full of opportunities, places to explore, museums to visit, groups to join. Knowing what to offer, what to keep in mind for another day and what to discard is a practised skill. This activity invites you to create a menu of the things that might be of interest to your child.

The menu could be linked specifically to an interest they have, or it could be a collection of local places to visit, or maybe a list of trips being organised by local home educators (see Figure 6.1). In this way you can create multiple menus, and I promise that they will all have a range of ideas on them.

Treating it as a menu reminds us that this is not a to-do list.

This is a list of possibilities, a list that you can offer ideas from, if and when appropriate.

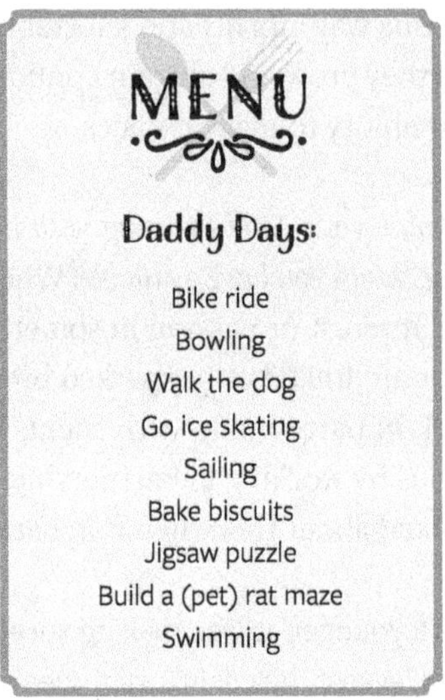

***Figure 6.1.** Ideas menu*

Dancing

Within school there is an inbuilt hierarchical system that exists between the child and the teacher. As the teacher holds all the keys to successfully passing the tests and achieving the targets set out for children, they are the ones who hold the power. The child has very little to no input. Unlike most other aspects of unschooling, it isn't a simple case of flipping this on its head and doing the direct opposite. While the child is now heavily involved and has complete agency in their education, it is not as straightforward as saying, 'We let the child do whatever they want'.

There is more. More than the adult being responsive to their child's needs. It is more than saying 'yes' to their every (possibly crazy) idea, more than making things possible for them, more than providing resources that they need or trips they want to go on, more than being present and engaging in their interests and conversations.

It isn't only about responding to their requests and following their interests; there is also scope for the adult to lead the way.

Dancing with your child means that sometimes you get to take the lead. What this looks like and how this is successful varies enormously. This means that we can make suggestions, introduce new ideas to our child, open up the world beyond their field of experience and contribute with our own questions and wonderings into a conversation.

It is not the same as setting out activities that you think your child *should* be doing. It is more akin to saying, 'I saw this and I thought of you', 'Here's a shell I found that we haven't seen before', 'Did you know there is an art gallery just up that road there?', 'A steam train is going to pass through the station on Saturday – shall we go and see it?', 'A new board game café has opened in the next town – shall we book a table?' 'The local Skywatchers are inviting people to come and use their telescopes to look at Jupiter tonight, what do you think of popping along?'

1. *There isn't a prescribed way of taking the lead; because we are in the habit of living in tune with our child, the way will depend on your child.* Some children need more direct invitations than others. You could find that you introduce a new sensory tray with slime in it and directly point it out to your child and they instantly have their hands in it and are away playing for the morning with something new. Another child might be put off by a verbal invitation but respond with interest if you are sat playing with the slime first. They may take time to watch with interest from a distance or ask questions about what it feels like or how far it can stretch before they join in themselves. Yet another child may ignore the tray of slime for days before they even poke one finger in it.

   Alice talked about how she navigates this dance with her daughter:

“I noticed if we're talking and a subject comes up, I think 'I'll explain this', and I'll get a sentence in, and my daughter will give me a look. And sometimes she'll say, 'Yeah, I've stopped listening now, Mum, you can stop explaining'. She is clear with me, and I listen and stop, because she's not interested. If she wants to know, she'll ask, 'Why does this work like this?' Or 'Why does that happen?'

Other times she'll ask questions about the world, and if I start commenting out loud on the news, then sometimes she'll want to know more about it. In this way, we have talked about British politics. She has thought through what it might take to be a good prime minister. She is interested in the world stage and how people are running things, and whether it's fair. That has largely come from discussion with me.

Introducing new ideas can feel more teacher-like than simply facilitating or partnering. The trick is to hold things lightly, offer invitations and suggestions with no expectation, and see the self-confidence and self-knowledge your child possesses when they are able to authentically say 'yes' or 'no' to those invitations.

2. Another way to lead the dance is to *introduce them to things that are currently outside of their scope*. Introduce interesting things into your home and make them aware of opportunities outside of the home too. Fill your home with curious things, artifacts, books, people, art. Put TV programmes or films that you find on to a wish list, unusual pictures on the wall, new words on the fridge door, interesting plants in the garden.

   Make your child aware of local home ed meet-ups, activities or classes. Talk about museum exhibitions or collections you know of or far-off places you can explore, either on holiday or via Google Earth. Keep introducing them to the wider world, beyond the borders of their own direct experience. Showcase what is out there and, as May Ling put it, share openly:

" There's a more physical part of unschooling. Providing them with opportunities and with resources and places to go and people to see, so that they're being exposed to stuff that maybe they're not finding themselves.

We've never had restrictions with their iPad. My eldest daughter had their first iPad when she was two because we were going on a plane to go and visit my sister. And I just thought, this is a good time. They have so much self-directed access to the world, right? But there's also the possibility that the world they're seeing is hugely curated by a Western criteria. And so there is also an element now in our environment of, what are you missing? And how do we provide it so that you have more information?

If it's important, something that I value and something that I would love you to know about, then how am I making sure that I am treating that like it's important? Not trying to push it onto them but helping cultivate this kind of openness to new stuff, to new input. Demonstrating that there are things that are important to us, too, by sharing that openly.

3. *Leading the dance can look like being curious and interested in life yourself.* It's rare to find an unschooling family that isn't led by adults who are curious by nature. Share your thoughts, questions, curiosity, awe and wonder at the world out loud. Be interested and interesting. Invest in your own joy and try out things that catch your eye. This is an excellent way to live in alignment with unschooling values as an adult. Be a lifelong learner and respond to your own needs, passions and ever-evolving knowledge. Your child may join in the questions and the search for answers, they may lend an ear and simply listen in, they may join in and learn a new craft or skill. As one friend said to me once, 'Run with sparkle'. And do it, not to be an example to your child, or with the intention that they will become interested or learn something about crochet or history or coppicing. Do it for you because it is a beautiful way to live. Lead with curiosity and **run with sparkle.**

Less teaching, more learning

The fact is that there is a difference between teaching and learning. What we are doing is creating a place in which our child can live and learn confidently and comfortably. We are creating homes, community and lives where curiosity is nurtured and learning can happen seamlessly. As the adult, we have an active role to play in our child's life so that learning can flourish, but that role is not as a teacher.

Teachers can never guarantee that their pupils are learning what they are being instructed to learn (try as they might). When we understand that learning belongs to the learner, that children will learn what they will, by providing a life that is fascinating and wonderous and responds to them as individuals, we can say that they are always learning and that that learning is deep and meaningful to them.

If we can grasp the difference between teaching and learning, we can also begin to grasp other differences too – intrinsic and extrinsic, stress and challenge, work and play, laziness and restfulness, parent and partner. As you move into partnership with your child, as you work with them to establish what it is that they need to be able to thrive, instead of 'letting the child do whatever they want', you are now in a position of 'helping the child to do whatever they want'. We can fully embrace the things that they embrace, in the ways that they embrace them. We can put the needed things in place to be able to support them when they need it, and step back and give them space when they need it.

In the times when you find yourself stepping back, because your child rejects your help, or shuns your input, or is exercising their wings and beginning to fly, there is always space to run with sparkle and embrace your own pursuits. Try new things, dive deeper into your passion, set yourself a challenge, follow your own line of questions and see where you end up, and have your own little learning adventure.

The result of this approach means that the natural curiosity that your child is born with is set ablaze rather than stamped out.

Principles to live by

- Make things easier for your child.
- Helping your child do what they want.
- Be generous.
- Be interested in what your child is doing.
- Run with sparkle.

Chapter 7

Reclaiming Childhood and Letting Children Play

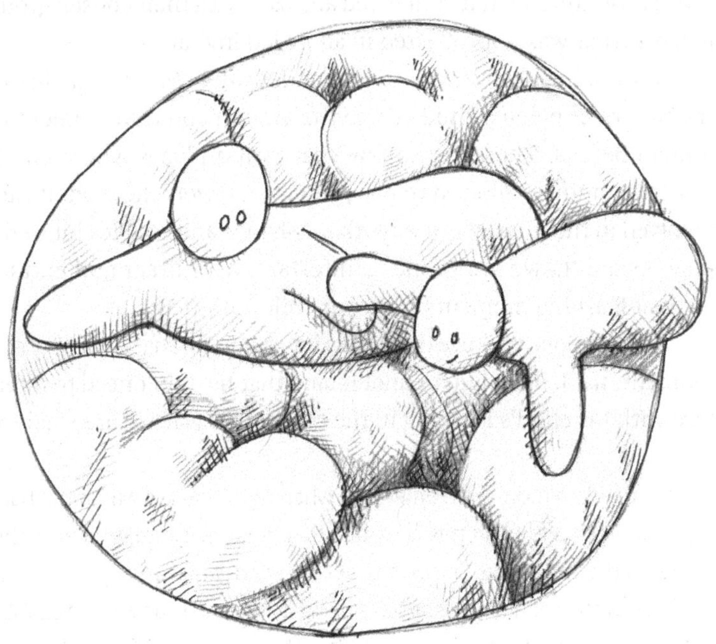

I am obsessed with children's play. From my beginnings as an Early Years teacher, it was evident to me that children who are immersed in play were learning deeply. There were other observations that I made too: the children were not learning what was prescribed for them, and intervening with my own agenda or removing them from their chosen activity to come and do some literacy or numeracy did more harm than good. I didn't know it at the time, but what I was observing and experiencing was self-determination theory, which you can read more about in Chapter 5. That is how children are motivated and how they are impacted by autonomy, competence and relatedness. Those children were motivated and engaged in their play in a way that, no matter how sparkly the activity, the adult-devised game did not reach the sweet spot for them (see Figure 5.4 and the 'Self-determination theory in action' exercise in Chapter 5). Those children felt confident and capable in their play in a way that was not replicated in adult-prepared activities (which focused and brought to the forefront the things a child could not do). Those children felt connected and safe with their chosen group in a way that was not reflected in adult-led invitations.

Play is a hugely overlooked and underrated essential quality to the nature of being a child and to the growth and development of human beings. There are so few spaces and places where children are genuinely allowed to play, and even fewer where adults are involved in those spaces in ways that enhance and enable children's play. As adults we are prone to interfere, overdirect and extract explicit learning moments from our children's play.

When I spoke to Steve during his interview, he shared a story of a moment that helped him to understand that he didn't need to interfere with his child's learning in the traditional way we are used to:

> " There was a moment I remember when my daughter was in the back of the car, and I had this fake idea that at some stage we'd probably learn the ABC song. She was about two-and-a-half and she sat in the back of the car and she started singing it. She had found it on YouTube and she knew it. Very quickly, she had three versions of the ABC song. She had one that ended in 'X Y Zed' and one that ended in 'X Y Zee'. And then she had her own version that was 'X, Y, Zed or Zee'. This is really sophisticated. I think that did a lot for me early on – and we have just let this continue to happen.

Being comfortable with letting that happen, letting your child explore and discover for themselves, organically learn things as they engage with the world around them on their own terms and join them where they are and play alongside them – this is different to the idea of play that dominates our world and the predisposition of well-meaning adults to interfere in unnecessary ways.

'Play-based learning' is not the same as genuine child's play. So not only do we suffer from not truly seeing what play looks like beyond the age of five, because of the interference of school, but play has also suffered from the corruption of dressing up teaching and adult-led activities as 'play'. This chapter is a celebration of play to encourage you to bring back play into your child's life. For those who worry that their child plays too much (even into adolescence), or for those whose children have never been to school and have not introduced 'school at home', this chapter is a brief look into the joys, practicalities and expectations of real play in childhood.

Essentially, play is the ultimate teacher, and all we do, as adults, is trust the process.

CONSIDERING THE JOY OF PLAY

Do you remember a time when you were young when you were playing a game? Maybe you were with friends or on your own? Maybe you were lying on the floor, sat at a table or running around the garden? Maybe you had toys like LEGO or a teddy bear, or maybe you had something you had found like sticks and mud? I wonder what feelings arise when you remember – warm, glowing feelings, joy and fondness, excitement and peace? I certainly hope that those are the sorts of memories you have.

Take a moment to think about that memory, take time to watch it, and to feel those feelings.

Now try and put into words that memory and those feelings. You could make a list, write prose, a poem or a world cloud.

When you think about choosing play over a curriculum for your own child, what thoughts, feelings and words come to mind? When you see your own child playing, spending their time doing the things they love, what thoughts are going through your head? Take another moment to articulate those words and feelings.

Put these two lists together and look at them side by side. What are the similarities and where are they different? It's helpful to identify where your concerns are if you have them, or the areas you would like to know more about to build your confidence in adopting play as the vehicle for optimal learning. Write down your concerns and questions as a separate list.

We have been duped. Ever so slowly over recent generations play has been twisted and turned, reshaped, repackaged, remastered and sold to us in a form that is so unrecognisable as play that we have failed to notice that it isn't. It's just like the wolf in sheep's clothing, or the sly fox in all those fairy tales that we hear. Right before our very eyes childhood has been gradually eroded, and now we have this warped perception of play and its purpose.

It is my hope that you will leave this chapter confident in your child's ability to learn through their play far beyond those early years, and maybe even **adopt a playful attitude** in your own life with abandon.

It's child's play: choosing to play

Anyone who works with children knows that if they are happy and engaged and find the activity interesting, then getting them to participate is easier, and learning happens because relaxed happy children means relaxed happy brains. The fewer stressors on the child equates to fewer barriers to their learning. Think of all those teachers and activity leaders who are constantly trying to make lessons 'engaging' for their pupils. The science company that is 'fun while educational', the drama group that 'brings learning to life' or the museum that offers 'interactive displays'. It's not a foreign concept. We know that when a child is genuinely enjoying the activity, the learning flows.

What we are asked to do in unschooling, instead of introducing play or fun into the activity of *our* choice, is to trust and know that there is learning and value in the things that your child chooses to play. Children have the capacity to decide what they find enjoyable and are learning while engaged in that activity. Instead of designing a fun way of teaching a new concept or practising a skill, know that they are learning in something they have initiated.

As May Ling pointed out in our chat together:

> “ We just didn’t introduce structure, the structure of nursery or of school, because it didn’t make any sense that that would add anything apart from stress and constriction.

So, instead of a curriculum or adult-initiated task, children can follow their own curiosity and explore the world on their own terms. This could be through many forms of play: imaginative play, physical play, creative play, social play, constructive play. It doesn’t matter what it is – if your child has chosen to do it, then there is something engaging for them in that activity, something they are learning.

The key indicators of time well spent and high engagement in the work that is being undertaken and games that are being played will be the fun, the excitement, the bright eyes, the deep immersion, the flow and lost time experienced. **Remember that play is important.**

These things stem from the fact the child has chosen what they are doing. They are interested in that activity, that process. They are driven by their internal compass to play that game. When given the opportunity to genuinely choose what they do, children will choose the thing that engages them in a way that suits them. Some children will choose dressing up and role-play, others will choose construction toys and building, some will prefer climbing trees and running around, others will simply want to tip over boxes of toys and tubs of pens (this counts as play too). It’s okay that they choose different things and interact with the world in different ways. The key to their connection with what they are doing and the heightened level of engagement is that they are doing it because they want to, and they are able to not do it when they decide that they are finished, or they have the freedom to move on or change the play as they need to.

Experiencing autonomy in their play increases their engagement, the learning is more meaningful and deeper connections are made. Making their own meaningful choices and being guided by their own intrinsic motivation to learn via their natural inclination to play makes a significant difference in how they experience learning, both now and in the future.

The frivolous nature of play

Often play is not seen as serious enough. We consider learning to be serious business, and play is considered a distraction from learning. The bottom line is that play and learning are viewed as two separate entities. I would argue, along with many who have gone before me, that play is, in fact, the work of childhood – play is serious business. Play openly challenges our modern-day definition of learning.

During their interview, Sorrel shared how they decide what is important and what their child should be doing:

> “Follow your kids. They'll tell you what they need. One of the big things is they only need to know what they need to know to be the age they are. My five-year-old only needs to know what a five-year-old needs to know to be five, which is not that much, really, and anything else that he does know he knows because it's interesting. My five-year-old doesn't need to worry about when he's 10, so I don't need to prepare him for when he's 10. Today is all we've got, this moment is the only thing that's guaranteed.

Play is often seen as frivolous, time wasting and silly. As a society play and learning have been distinguished in schools by timetabling separate playtime and lesson time. This echoes into adulthood as hobbies, relaxation and self-care become distinct from working hours and epitomised in the grind of Monday to Friday followed by the release of the weekend.

Play often acquires these descriptors when a child immerses themself in the same activity for too long or doesn't appear to be playing anything for a significant amount of time, when they don't finish what they started or don't even have a plan. And let's not forget if they are laughing too much, or the play has taken a turn, and frivolity ends with extended fits of giggles. In short, adults tend to apply a work-based ethic to learning and fail to see the point or the outcome of play.

Because play is a process-orientated endeavour it is often seen as time wasting and unproductive. This is the opposite to being product-orientated and is one of the reasons why it challenges our definition and experience of learning, especially outside the school system. So much of what we orchestrate as learning – classes, tutors, lessons, curriculum, activities – is driven by an outcome or a final product. There is an aim to the session. In schools, lessons are prefaced with a 'learning outcome', personal reviews at the end of lessons are a reflection on what has been learned, progress is tracked via concrete evidence using worksheets and tests, and extra-curricular activities lead to awards and certificates in celebration of recognised progress.

Play is rarely about the end result or the product. The focus doesn't tend to be the completed project, the finished piece of artwork or setting out to remember all the facts about each Pokémon card. Children engage in an activity because they love it, or they want to try it, or they are enjoying the feeling of rolling around in the mud, or they are excited by the exploding coke – it is playing for playing's sake. There is no agenda, it just is. They are driven by the desire that they have in the moment to do what they are doing. And while they are doing what they are doing they are acquiring skills and making connections between all the things they know, the things they thought they knew, and the things they know now. They learn through the process of playing – not by setting themselves a target or outcome, but simply by doing it.

The reality of play

The truth is that play is messy, both literally and metaphorically. The physical mess can be just as difficult to manage as the metaphorical mess. It is chaotic, it appears nonsensical. Nothing about play is linear or clean and tidy in the ways we have become accustomed to.

The physical mess created by children's play can be frustrating and become unmanageable. Their desire to make mud pies that results in a muddy garden and children covered in clay, potion making with bowls filled with grass and petals and water poured in pools around bottles that will stagnate over time, painting sessions that evolve into full body rolling in paint or painting the walls, jumping in puddles when they don't have welly boots on, running into the sea fully clothed or finding the entire bathroom supplies emptied on the bathroom floor. This physical mess is one of the ways that play can push us as adults out of our comfort zone, especially when we are left with the clear-up. It also leaves us with a desire to manage the mess and prevent it happening again.

If you can **make time for play** and resist the urge to constantly tidy up, this will benefit how your child plays and how they access their toys and activities. Leaving the doll's house mid-game and not resetting the pieces means that play can easily continue when they return. Leaving the paints out on the table when it appears they have finished (for now) means that they can come back to them with ease. Keeping the home-made den in the corner of the room eases the return to the space. There are times when things may need to be put away, but having open shelving or clear boxes so that children can readily see and access their toys can also help with the flow of their play.

Making play possible for your child is part of unschooling, enabling them to do the things they want to and facilitating what they need. As Alice described in our conversation:

> “Taylor was originally in burnout. She was pretty much shut in her room with an iPad, demanding ice, demanding drinks, demanding snacks, sweets and watching TV. She didn't want anyone in there. Didn't want to do anything. So when she started to be able to spend more time and sit and play and get involved in an activity, I would do everything as she asked me too. Whether that's setting up the pieces or putting the pieces away, I'll organize everything, just to make it easier. It's facilitating, that's your job. That's all the things you're told as a parent not

to do, because you're told that you are 'giving in to them' and 'you're making life too easy for them'.

With a neurodivergent child, those sorts of things just add to that sense of overwhelm, which mean they never get to explore these things because it's just too hard. So having me there, setting things up, keeping it neat, keeping it organized, helping her with that, that's when I started to notice her spending more time playing. This happened fairly soon after we deregistered and the expectation to go to school was removed.

Metaphorically speaking play rarely makes sense to the adult gaze. We have become accustomed to the linear progression of learning. Curriculums that are preset for us in a step-by-step fashion have formatted learning for us. The reality of what play looks like is an alien concept for many. We don't know where it is going to go or what is going to happen next, and each child is different. Some children constantly flit in their play from one activity or game to another; others play the same thing for hours or even days on end. Other children don't even appear to be doing anything that resembles play and can appear destructive, illogical or even sedentary, and we cannot make sense of what they are doing and learning right now, let alone consider how what they are doing is going to change into something more constructive.

Teenagers can often be found playing in their own ways. It can look like organised games, but it can also look like silliness, play fighting, joining in chase with younger children, delving into make-believe and gaming. It can be disconcerting to see our teenagers playing in ways that schooled teens have little opportunity to; it often makes little sense to us, but it is part of the rich tapestry of how they make sense of the world and find their place in it. And maybe we could benefit from taking a leaf out of their book and find ways to play more and do so with abandon.

While we might be able to manage some of the physical mess that occurs, we cannot control the metaphorical mess. We cannot and should not control our children's learning. Unlike mainstream education where a teacher sets out the targets and learning outcomes of any given lesson, here it is the child who chooses, and this is not often done consciously. It is an essential element of play that it is self-chosen and self-directed, that the child chooses to be there and that they can choose when to move on. As soon as we step in and insist that they must play a game by our rules, that they should finish the picture they started or bake the cake themselves, a shift happens – we change the dynamic and it moves away from the child's natural mode of operation. This then changes the relationship with the activity and impacts the learning that is occurring, and it is almost always an unnecessary interjection.

The power of play: beyond the Early Years

As if that wasn't enough, unschooling asks us to continue to nurture our child's inclination to play beyond the age of five. While their peers are donning school uniforms and being introduced to reading programmes, minute-by-minute timetables and structured learning, unschooled children do not choose those things. Children who live a life without school continue to choose to play much in the same way that they have done up until this point.

Their play might change, they may introduce new things, their games become more complex, but typically children who are provided with swathes of time to engage with the world on their own terms and in their own way will continue to play. Having spent over a decade in the unschooling community, I have observed that it is common to see children playing right up until adolescence. And even then, it doesn't disappear entirely; it is evident that young people can and will play with their peers and in mixed age groups both confidently and happily.

What this means is that children are not acquiring knowledge and facts in the same way that their schooled peers might be doing. They are not necessarily purposefully learning to read, they refuse imposed, direct instruction as they become confident in their own self and the decisions that they make, and their approach to finding things out is significantly less straightforward without having to use a prescriptive method. Also, they often actively choose the fun, frivolous and chaotic over the serious, structured and measurable.

What they are doing, though, is setting themselves up for a lifetime of learning. Play involves a great many skills that are transferable across all areas of life. Meta skills that are unobtrusively developed, rehearsed and built while our children play on their own terms. Skills that will hold them in good stead throughout their lives. When we observe our children's play closely, we see them using skills like researching, hypothesising, questioning, negotiation, evaluating, categorising and organising, as well as a whole lot more.

They might not be wholly evident but let's take a look at a few examples together, in Figure 7.1.

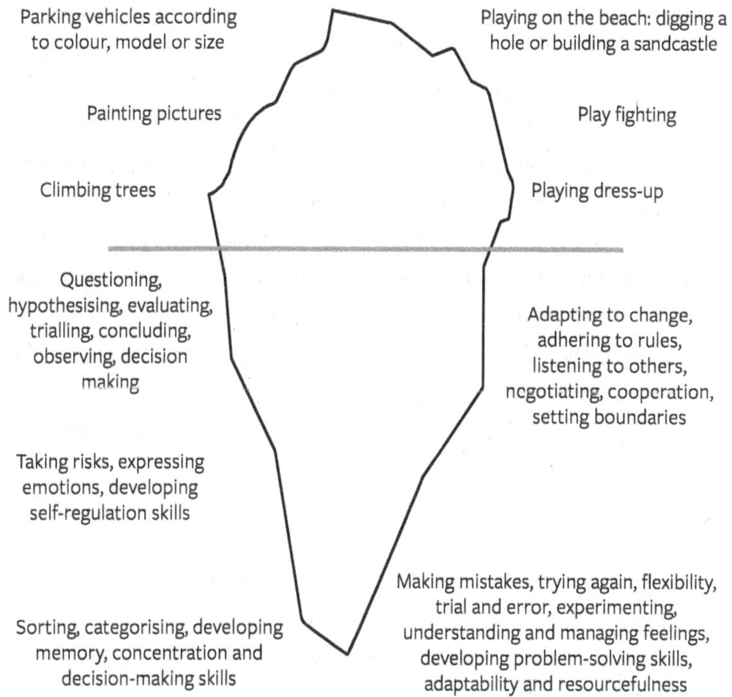

Figure 7.1. *Some skills developed through play*

The problem is that unless we are purposefully looking for these things, then what we tend to see is the surface-level fun, frivolous and messy aspects of play. The meta skills that are being developed are a core aspect of our ability as adults to manage life well and cultivate an attitude towards learning that establishes it as a lifelong endeavour. We often call these life skills. Again, this is not a list of practical things that you are able to do, like change a light bulb or read a bus timetable, but your approach and response to life events big and small includes learning how to learn.

Alice described how her daughter practised and developed skills through her play in ways that she wasn't afforded in her schooling – remember that her daughter was nine when she first deregistered from school:

> “We spent hours talking about which Sylvanian characters she wanted, which families she wanted to play with. It struck me how much time she needed for even the smallest decision and all those things that you would rush them through. And I mean, at school, you wouldn't have a fraction of the time to decide on things.
>
> When you watch it playing out in such depth, the minutiae of making those decisions and talking about it, it's been fascinating watching that in slow motion, and under the microscope.
>
> 'If I do this, then I can do this, but the opportunity cost is that I don't get to do this, but I want to do that, and all of those. I can't have my cake and eat it. So what do I do?'
>
> And rather than just say, 'Well, you just have to get used to the fact you can't have both', it's way more complex.
>
> After days, she'll try rolling a dice, doing a kind of random decision making. She'll get me to decide and then say, 'No, that's not what I want.' We choose the one behind the back, all sorts of things that were just not satisfactory.
>
> I've got that time and I've got the patience then to not get frustrated with her for not deciding and to watch her doing those steps through those processes and voicing it and definitely finding it easier as time's gone on.

And even better news is that these skills are being developed across all manner of ways that children play. So it makes no difference whether your child is interested in cars, or dinosaurs, or dressing up, or riding a bike, dancing, gaming, painting, or watching TV series, or anything else. These skills are being used across all aspects of children's play, and importantly, they are transferable. This means that they are the same skills they will need as they grow and begin to experiment and incorporate new interests, ideas, games and pastimes into their repertoire. They may look ill developed and immature during this period of time, but their play offers them the chance to get better at them in conjunction with their own developmental pathways.

Playfulness

There isn't a moment when play becomes what we may identify as more serious learning. There may be moments where you see something that looks familiar to you and reassuring that 'serious learning' is happening, something that is less chaotic and more purposeful or academic.

During adolescence the brain goes through some enormous amounts of rewiring, and as part of that we can often observe a shift away from the childlike form of play towards something that is more akin to explicit learning. Again, this doesn't happen overnight, and I am about to argue that it maintains much playfulness in its approach, that is, that we can see how the skills developed through their play evolve into essential components of the learning they are now undertaking. Table 7.1 explores the various attributes and defining characteristics of play and how they change beyond the age of five and through into adolescence, providing insights into how different types of play contribute to overall growth and learning.

Table 7.1. Defining characteristics of play: from young child through to adolescent

Play	Beyond the age of five	Through adolescence
Play is self-chosen and self-directed	Children choose what they want to play and how they want to play	Levels of autonomy are high, and young people continue to be able to opt in and out
Play is an activity in which the means are more valued than the end	Playing for play's sake is the primary motivator – having fun and enjoying what they are doing. The process continues to be important, but the end result becomes a growing consideration	The approach to the activity and the process is one of curiosity and discovery, often as a means to completing a set project
Play has structure and rules	The activity chosen has recognised and valued structure and rules	Young people recognise the structures and limitations as well as challenge the rules, and collaborate and negotiate with those involved in the task
Play is imaginative, non-literal, mentally removed in some way from 'real' life	Activities include those that reflect the real world but are removed in some way, e.g. using dolls to play 'going to the play park'	Being able to imagine the next steps, think through potential barriers, and visualise clients and the audience is an imaginative process
Play involves an alert but non-stressed frame of mind	They choose activities they continue to find fun and engaging	Young people enjoy what they are doing, are personally invested in the activity and are challenged by the work they are undertaking

Source: Adapted from Peter Gray's definition of play[1]

1 Gray, Peter (2008) 'The value of play I: The definition of play gives insights.' *Psychology Today*, Blog, 19 November. www.psychologytoday.com/us/blog/freedom-learn/200811/the-value-play-i-the-definition-play-gives-insights

Making meaningful choices

When our children have been given the opportunity to constantly and consistently make autonomous choices, they continue to do so. This means that they make decisions based on meeting their needs and developing their interests. As young people develop this often means that they are better at identifying groups and places that suit their needs before they join, but they are also great at leaving spaces that aren't equipped to meet those needs.

Alice describes the process that her daughter, aged 12, and two years out of school, goes through when she is exploring a new activity or group:

> " I mentioned a gymnastics class that was drop-in, so she thought she'd give that a go.
>
> We'll have a look. If she doesn't want to go in, we don't go in. If she doesn't want to stay, we don't stay. Constantly checking in. And she would want to go back each week, because we carefully added it, and she'd put a lot of thought into it. Always going through this decision-making process of, 'Do I want to add another activity? Do I not want to add another activity? Is it going to be too many people? Is it going to be too much stress?' And all along, having those conversations about how much is too much for her, and when she gets overwhelmed, and whether it'll be too noisy.
>
> Each of these activities and events have previously been a struggle to get to. There have been times that she can't get up, she can't get dressed, she can't do her teeth, she can't get out of the door. Now they are no problem at all. Each of those activities she chose if she wanted to go, and she'd be up and out the door, and we'd never have any trouble.
>
> Every few weeks or a couple of months we added another activity. I'd drop these ideas in there, I noticed that there's a drama group or whatever, and they meet on whatever days, and she'd pretty much ignore me. But then a few weeks later, a couple of months later, just say, 'I think I'd like to try that'. And then we'd give it a go. And these days, she's doing a different class every day.

It often also means that their interests become narrower and increasingly defined. For some children this is consistently true from a young age, but for others this can be the stage where they invest more time in fewer areas of interest. Or it may manifest itself in the depth of knowledge and passion in a range of topics or activities.

Competence and capability

There is a significant shift in the way that young people approach their activities during adolescence. Again, this is not an instant shift that happens overnight, but a gradual change that ebbs and flows. Alison Gopnik, a developmental psychologist, describes the difference between these two phases, from the early years of 'discovery' to developing 'mastery' learning.[1]

Play is predominantly process-based; there is little defined purpose other than to engage in the activity for the fun of it. Children play for play's sake, and in this immersive state there is discovery in each moment. This changes as children get older; it becomes apparent that they sometimes do choose to do a task because they want to achieve a set outcome. This can be seen when children set out to learn to swim, complete a stop motion video or perfect the drawing of an eye. It is probably most obvious when they set out to take an exam or pursue a career. The result, that is, the product, becomes the intention.

Mastery learning is forced on to children at a very young age within schools. The completion of a piece of work or set project is highly valued (think of all the children who have to miss playtime in order to finish their work). Yet children who have not been to school make the shift from one to the other without formal instruction to do so.

One of the things that is noticeable with unschooled children is that the *process* of getting to the final product remains important. The process remains enjoyable, even when challenging; mistakes are

1 Gopnik, Alison (2016) *The Gardener and the Carpenter: What the New Science of Child Development Tells Us About the Relationship Between Parents and Children*. Farrar, Straus and Giroux.

part of the learning and not shameful problems; and their internal motivation is high even though the reward may be something external and not immediate once they reach the mastery phase.

Connection with others

Play is often a social endeavour. It requires guidelines and 'rules' that are formed and adhered to by the group. It is a safe place to experiment with those rules and test what happens when they are changed. This develops an understanding of how working within the rules is necessary in certain situations, but children also have the confidence to challenge and change the rules where they need to. The use of imagination and collectively trying out ideas allows them to consider the context in which they are creating a product, marketing their goods, writing a story and performing a show, as they can imagine themselves in the place of the customer, reader or audience accordingly – all the while being attuned to the difference between being challenged and engaged in their choices, finding fun, purpose and enjoyment in their life's work, but not being stressed or understimulated.

While play is predominantly the work of childhood, and provides an essential growth and development route into adulthood, it never truly disappears. Life retains playfulness, and the skills, attitude and intent of true play develop and evolve into key elements that contribute to a happy and healthy adulthood – autonomy, engagement, challenge, imagination, positive social interaction – without the shame, stress and restriction, as Sally described when I asked her if she could have predicted the things that her eldest is doing now when they started unschooling:

> "I saw some of it. I see their interests are the same as when they were eight: politics, economics, the world, linguistics, languages. They're still talking about the same things they've been talking about for eight years.
>
> I couldn't have imagined what my 18-year-old was capable of, though. His ability to be with groups, to put himself out there, how he has tackled his social anxiety. It has been really amazing to watch, even though it's still hard. I feel like unschooling for him has been amazing, because it's allowed him to go at his own pace and to choose the place

he wants to be. He hasn't had to go through extreme discomfort to get to this point, and he now does all sorts of things. He takes on these challenges, at his own pace, and that's allowed him to become much more confident. I think that's been one of the most remarkable things.

Play for as long as possible, and then play some more

If I could encourage you to do one practical thing for your child, it would be to **create space in the day for them to play**, genuinely play. The more time that they play, the more optimal their development and learning in a holistic and healthy way. Of course, if they have lost their playful roots this may take time, gradual change, purposeful direction and creating a new family culture, but it is possible. You can revisit Chapters 3 and 4 and devise a plan for your family.

When we talk about unschooling as natural learning we need to seriously consider how children naturally are, to provide them with space to be who they are and to do the things that children do. Children need space to play and lots of it, and they need to be able to do it in ways that suit them. It's invaluable to their understanding of themselves and the world. It's invaluable to the opportunity it gives them to process big ideas and real-life experiences in a safe and self-managed environment. For children, time spent playing is time well spent.

And remember that, in among the fun, frivolous, chaotic and messy nature of play, there is some serious learning going on.

Principles to live by

- Adopt a playful attitude.
- Remember that play is important.
- Make time for play.
- Create space in the day for them to play.

Chapter 8

How Children Learn to Read in the Real World

Susan has two children with quite different stories to share about how they learned to read. When I spoke to her, she told me about her eldest child's experience when he started school:

> He was always very interested in stories, always interested in books and reading. He loved the *Alphablocks* TV series and was massively into that way before he went to school. So he automatically had a grounding in phonics even from that, without me ever teaching any phonics. He was just starting to build letter sounds and build words before he went to school. Unfortunately, because of the challenges that he has, school was a traumatic and really very negative experience for him, and during the three years he did at school, he literally stopped reading. They couldn't get him to read at the time we had finished and pulled him out to home educate.

This is a story that I hear frequently in my work supporting families as they unschool their children. The joy of reading has been sucked away by a child's school experience to such an extent that even reading for functional purposes is avoided. The trauma surrounding their experience has a negative effect on the child's ability to engage in reading.

I have also witnessed in my teaching career the negative effect that persistently and relentlessly requiring children to work through different reading programmes and sit through additional reading classes has on them. Being removed from subjects that they often excel at or love, like art, science and sport, so that they can spend more time doing more of the thing that they hate. It's no wonder that their enthusiasm for reading wains when their experience is one of difficulty, humiliation and shame.

Susan's younger child never went to school and has been unschooled for his entire education:

> Interestingly, he has never been a child that is particularly drawn to stories. I have and did read to him, but he was never that interested. He loved music and other things but not particularly stories, but we did read to him.

I asked Susan what gave her the confidence to take an unschooling approach with her eldest when it came to learning to read. Here is what she had to say:

> All the research that I had done around unschooling and self-directed education, and trauma, I knew that, I trusted that his love of reading would win through, providing we took the pressure off and allowed him to heal. So when he came out of school, I absolutely did not mention reading at all.

And by the time her youngest became school age:

> Having had quite a few years of unschooling and read quite widely about how these children in this environment can learn, I felt comfortable trusting the process. That because he was immersed in language, and because reading was widely used in the family, that it would be something that he would develop in his own pace and his own way. I trusted that giving him a rich environment would get him there at the time that was right for him.

Trusting the process

'Trust the process' – I wonder if that's something you have heard before as you have been finding out more about unschooling. It sounds a little bit like trying to catch smoke! What does it even mean? And how do you trust a process that you know nothing about and what do you actually do? Susan gives us some clues in her interview – there were some things she was actively doing, and things that unschooling parents do all the time that enable a child to confidently direct their lives and learn in their own time and in their own way.

It is not the same as working to a curriculum when we put our trust in the method or scheme that is being used. Curriculums give us confidence because they give us a road map of what to do and how to do it with a guaranteed outcome that your child will learn to read. As many adults and children have experienced, it also has other outcomes, doesn't guarantee that every child will learn to read at the young age of five, and, from an unschooling perspective, interferes with the principle that children can and will learn what they need to, when they need to.

Enabling your child to learn something in their own time and in their own way is not the same as doing nothing. We might not be using reading schemes or workbooks or explicitly teaching them, but there are things that we are doing. We don't leave them to it and hope that they pick it up. I don't have a road map to give you for what it will look like for your child (that's where you will be trusting the process), but there are important things that you can and probably are already doing that will pave the way for your child to learn to read.

This isn't a recipe just for children learning to read. These are components by which children learn anything – maybe it's reading but it could be maths, or science, or writing. It could easily be Pokémon, trains, tumbling or acrylic art. The combination of these key elements works together to enable our children to learn anything that they need to.

Whether your child is recovering from negative associations about reading that they acquired from their schooling, or you have been locked in a battle at home because they don't seem to be 'getting it', or don't want to engage with phonics, worksheets or reading at all, or you are fully invested in an unschooling life and ready to know more about how children learn to read without school – this is the chapter for you!

How children learn to read in school

As an Early Years teacher and having worked extensively with children who have English as an additional language (EAL), I have taught hundreds of children to read. When children enter the school system at the age of four, most are unable to read, and while Reception classes are largely play-based environments, there is an early focus on reading, writing and maths. Unsurprisingly, these are frequently the subjects that cause the most concern for parents when they are considering home education, and certainly when adopting a self-directed learning approach.

Children in schools begin specific reading lessons the moment they walk through the door. There are reading schemes and phonics systems widely used in classrooms that can take children from non-readers to readers within six weeks. Parents are instructed to listen to their child read every night and complete home-school reading logs. Children are sent home with phonics work sheets and accompanying 'high frequency words' to learn. Some schools offer parent meetings where they explain how the programme works and what is expected of the parents, children and school, for everyone to be using the same approach.

You may be familiar with a phonics-based approach, whereby children are taught the sound that a single letter, pairing or group of letters make. These are then used like building blocks to both break down and build up a word to be able to read it.

It hasn't always been this way. For years there has been an ongoing debate about the best way to learn to read. Using a 'whole word'-based approach was popular some years back, possibly when you yourself went to school. This approach can be seen when tools like flashcards are used or cutting out words following the shape of the letters that construct the word. Some schools use a hybrid method that incorporates this approach when teaching high frequency words, spelling tests or interventions for dyslexic children.

Both these approaches give the impression that reading is a concerted and arduous task that must be undertaken and endured. Learning to read is actually no different from learning to care for your pet, how to plant and grow beans, or all the words to your favourite song. I'm fairly sure you don't worry about those things, and you have a good idea of how you would help your child to do them if they wanted to.

You have learned to worry about your child's reading because of school.

The earlier the better (for schools)

For schools it is necessary for children to be able to read even at a basic level so that the delivery of lessons, evidence of learning and record keeping are made easier when working with large groups of children. It is the perfect example of a system that is put in place for the benefit of the system and the adults implementing it. Children are taught to read because it benefits the process of teaching the curriculum throughout the rest of their school years.

It is inevitable when you insist on investing in an approach to teaching reading (or anything else), at a specific age, that you will have children for whom it doesn't work. One size does not fit all. Children are not machines you can programme with certain instructions at a certain age and expect them all to have the same results. Humans are more complex than that.

> “Meet Robert.
>
> He is eight years old and not keen on reading.
>
> He finds it really hard and is slow at reading words on a page, even with help.
>
> He has been learning phonics in different ways for four years and the stories in the reading schemes are for much younger children.
>
> Robert is often taken out of classes that he loves so that he can spend more time doing this thing that he has come to loathe.
>
> He has lost any interest in reading for pleasure, there is no joy in books, and he now has a barrier to reading as he feels like it isn't something that he can do.
>
> He is singled out in the classroom and other children exclude him. Children in Robert's position often experience this as trauma.

There are thousands of children just like Robert who don't enjoy reading, no longer want to do it and have a poor view of themselves and their ability to learn. This is the side effect of such rigid approaches: children who are seen as failures by the time they are in Year 1 (at 5–6 years old). And it isn't their fault. Not all children are ready to be readers at the age of four, but that doesn't mean they will never be able to read.

As adults we have come to believe that if children aren't explicitly taught to read, they won't ever be able to, and that learning to read at a young age is normal and vital. Reading, like everything else, is part of a broader picture. It is part of our ability to communicate and is intricately linked to writing, conversation and other methods of communicating. Not only that, but did you know that your child's physical development is also related to their ability to read?

We often think about learning to read as reading books together, or maybe we branch out further and see literacy all around us in written form. Rarely do we value going to the play park, climbing trees, riding a scooter or dancing as games that support your child's ability to read. Trusting that what your child is doing right now (in this case, being a physically active child) is equipping them for what they need to do in the future (being able to read) turns what we believe about education upside down.

Your child is busy doing all the things that they need to do; the trick is for you to facilitate and trust that. Hold back the panic and desire to intervene, redirect or introduce activities specifically for the purpose of *teaching* your child to read. Meeting your child's needs now and providing them with what they need today, to do the things they want to do, that is how you prepare them to do the things they want to do in the future. **Meeting current needs meets future needs.**

Your child might pick up reading at the age of four, but more likely they will be throwing some moves on the trampoline or digging a hole in the garden. Quite possibly they could be flicking through their library books while on the trampoline or looking at a book about the earth while digging a hole. It all weaves together in the end.

Learning to read without school

When our children are immersed in life they have a context for their learning that is meaningful to them. Learning to read is a cultural process for self-directed learners; it has significance and purpose that is decided on by the learner. Harriet Pattison, Senior Lecturer in Early Childhood Studies at Liverpool Hope University, has published studies on how children learn to read without school, and introduces us to this idea of the cultural process rather than a cognitive one.[1]

What does this mean? The cognitive process is illustrated in school methods where the skill of reading is taught and taught

1 Pattison, Harriet D. A. (2014) 'Rethinking learning to read: The challenge from children educated at home.' Thesis, University of Birmingham. www.academia.edu/68799100/Rethinking_learning_to_read_the_challenge_from_children_educated_at_home

sequentially. The cultural process focuses on how the child views themself and their role as an important member of their family and wider community. We are all familiar with the idea that children should love reading, particularly fiction books, but when we begin to understand the wider context of acquiring this skill and its broader role in our society, we can begin to see how children learn to read organically with our support.

Children learn other skills, without instruction, that are culturally grounded too. Both walking and talking are significantly difficult skills to acquire, and yet those children who can, do so. Adults have a role to play to help children develop these skills, but it is not the one of a teacher. Being in tune with your child, being responsive to your child's questions, providing them with the answers and being prepared to be flexible centres the learner and their relationship with those around them. The idea that **relationship comes first** permeates throughout unschooling, even as far as our children learning to read.

Harriet Pattison also discovered that it was possible for a child to live in a family immersed in literacy and reading, including regularly sharing in read-aloud practices, where the child didn't learn to read until their teen years. Parents also reported that their children learned to read in different ways – not only were the accounts different between families, but also between the children within those families.

Her research isn't the only study that highlights self-directed learners coming to reading on their own a lot later than is required within schooling. Peter Gray has also published insights that show that children can learn to read, and read well, anywhere between the ages of 4 and 14, and for many of these children there is no underlying difficulty.[1]

Commonly held beliefs around learning to read (which can be equally applied to writing or numeracy) are significantly challenged by those who learn outside of the school system. Remember Susan's

1 Gray, Peter (2010) 'Children teach themselves to read.' *Psychology Today*, Blog, 24 February. www.psychologytoday.com/gb/blog/freedom-to-learn/201002/children-teach-themselves-to-read

eldest child who shut down to the idea of reading entirely? I think that we know that within school he would have been pressured to persevere, probably in the name of resilience, accompanied by targets, tracking and testing. Susan did something unschool-like, though. It was this step back that relieved the pressure, provided her son with the space to heal, and to reengage with the process on his own terms that enabled him to learn to read and, as we will discover, enjoy doing it.

Table 8.1 outlines some of the ways in which learning to read works without school. It takes some common approaches that are used within mainstream schooling and then provides an unschooling way to approach it instead.

Table 8.1. Ways that learning to read works without school

Instead of:	The unschooling way is to:	Which has the result of:
Using a standardised programme...	Notice how we are culturally surrounded by literacy (including reading)	Understanding that learning to read is an unavoidable part of life!
Doing what the curriculum tells you to...	Respond to your child's questions and natural desire to learn	Allowing them to come to reading in their own time, being fully supported along the way
Assessing their reading level and only giving them access to books that are 'appropriate'...	Say 'yes!' to any book or reading material that interests them	Giving them access to a range of genres and meaningful reading material
Raising the importance of reading above other learning...	Embrace whatever they are learning right now and recognise that reading will happen when the time is right for your child	Removing the pressure and expectation, therefore removing stress, maintains a clear and easy path to learning to read, when your child is ready
Separating reading from other subjects...	Live, play, work and learn seamlessly	Children often acquiring the skills they need to read in ways we don't recognise and are often undetected by us and by them

That last one might seem a bit unhelpful. We all want to see it happening, right? For our own peace of mind. It would be helpful to be able to tick off which phonics your child knows or if they can read a common word. Unschooling is not measurable in the same way that schooled approaches are. This is why 'trusting the process' is a useful principle to keep in mind.

No one said it would be easy.

I do have an idea on how to make it more comfortable, though. The next section lays out five ways that you can actively help your child to learn to read as an unschooling parent.

The ABC of learning to read in the real world

Children have all the tools they need within themselves to be able to learn to read. Direct teaching, reading programmes or a trained adult, pressure and force only diminish the quality and use of those tools. There are a few things that will help and support them on their discovery of reading. I have narrowed it down to five essential ingredients that children need to be able to learn to read as unschoolers (see Figure 8.1). Each has an important role to play in learning to read and all are easy to access.

That's right: No training certificate needed!

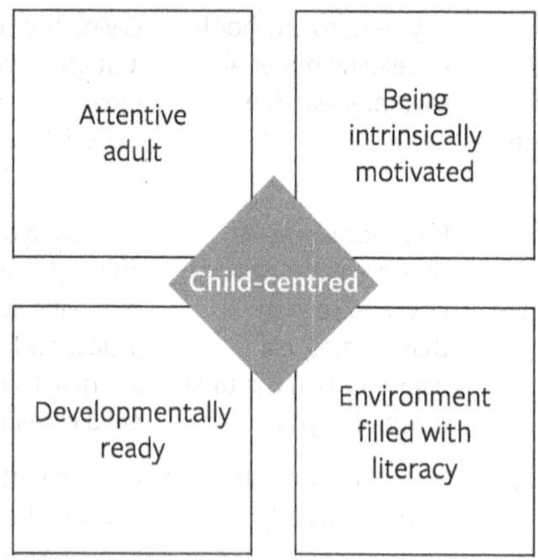

Figure 8.1. *The ABC of learning to read the unschooling way*

A is for attentive adult

“Meet Zain.

Zain is eight years old and unschooled.

He loves listening to a wide variety of stories.

His mum reads to him every night. They are currently reading *The Hobbit*.

He is allowed to choose any book that he wants from the library.

Right now, he is unable to read for himself, but he is relaxed about this and feels no pressure or sense of failure.

He won’t read for himself for another four years (at 12 years old) and his mum will continue reading bedtime stories to him for another six years (at 14 years old).

Zain has a designated adult to support him to learn. Some children have more than one adult, sometimes even an entire community, that come alongside them in their learning and respond to their questions and curiosities. Learning to read doesn’t start with deciphering letters on a page or recognising words. It begins long before that with language, talking with our children, singing songs, lullabies, nursery rhymes and everyday conversation. It can be listening to audio books, watching TV programmes or films. It can be being read to every night, being taken to the library, having access to magazines, information books, recipes, reading leaflets together or even road signs.

It needs an adult who is paying attention, providing what the child needs, responding to their questions. An adult who reads words for them, takes an interest in what they are discovering, who gently experiences life from their child’s perspective. It also takes an adult who can confidently say ‘yes’ to their questions and individual requests. Zain’s parents could easily say that a book such as *The Hobbit* is too big for an eight-year-old who can’t yet read themself. They could say that it is too grown-up for him too, or they could use it as a motivational tool and say that he can’t have it until he can read for himself. His parents have stepped away from all these commonly held ideas and relaxed into listening to what Zain has asked for and shown interest in. In this way the world of literature opens up to him, and he is able to explore its possibilities freely and discover what is there, with an attentive and supportive adult by his side.

There is a wonderful dynamic among unschooled children too, ones who are fully trusted with their own lives and learning. I have witnessed for myself how they support each other without any fan fair or drama; it is just the way that they are with each other. I have watched older children struggle to read the instructions for a new game that they have downloaded with a group of friends. I have heard them explain that they can't read as fast as everyone else and without hesitation their younger friends offering to read it for them. I have heard children asking their friends how to spell certain words while playing online together and they casually spell out the word that is needed. I have watched best friends decoding words together for treasure hunts and laughing together when messages they have written to each other don't make sense and then tell each other what the message actually says. When our children live without shame and judgement and are genuinely supported they have the means to access reading without shrinking away from it.

B is for being intrinsically motivated

As an unschooling family, intrinsic motivation is an active ingredient – personal interest, making their own choices and being naturally curious about the world are essential qualities for learning anything. **Personal drive enables learning.** With a personal need to learn something, that thing becomes much easier to grasp, and in the case of reading, provides a reason to do it, especially for those who learn to read in their teenage years.

Susan's interview outlines how both her boys learned to read because of their interest in gaming. This is not an uncommon story among unschooling families. The need to read instructions, daily challenges, details and statistics – this provides a reason to figure out the words in front of you. This can mean the child asking someone to read the text for them, it can mean them observing the buttons you select when they tell you what they need you to do, it can mean them sitting and trying to decode the words for themself.

The first words my children read confidently were 'pause', 'play', 'Minecraft' and 'Zombie'!

During my interview with Susan, she recalled how her eldest rediscovered his love of reading:

> "His love of story is the thing that has really driven his comeback and return to reading. He absolutely loves Japanese anime, and he was religiously watching all the episodes that were dubbed into English. Then he ran out of episodes that were dubbed into English, and he asked me for subtitled and access to subtitled versions. I didn't say anything, I just gave him access to a digital subscription to anime knowing full well that he had to be reading the subtitles if he was going to be understanding it, because it was going to be all said in Japanese. And then literally, after hundreds and hundreds of episodes of anime, he then started asking me for the written art form manga; he has had digital subscriptions for that, he has had volumes of that and he has run all the way [through] hundreds and thousands of episodes of manga, and then he suddenly said, 'Mum there's these things called manga light novels, could you get me some?' So we started to get those on Kindle and physical volumes, and now he is fully fluently reading what we would see as age-appropriate reading having never had any formal teaching since he left school. And in fact, school had an incredibly negative impact on his reading journey. But again, trusting, I mean he not only reads manga, but he's also hugely into blog accounts and reading other people's reviews of manga, so through the love of story, following his passion and researching all of that and reading all of these reviews, and everything else, that's what has driven his return to reading.

It makes a noticeable difference to learning to read and their attitude towards it when your child is personally driven. It doesn't mean that it might not be frustrating at times, or that they won't get things wrong, but it's much easier to keep trying when you are intrinsically motivated.

C is for child-centred

Your child is different to every other child there is or ever will be. The way your child learns to read will be their own unique journey. Without listening to and observing your child and responding respectfully to them, learning to read is likely to cause a struggle. If you try to replicate techniques from shared stories, and do things the same way as others have, without it being appropriate for your child, it will be a difficult task. If you actively try to 'do' anything to your child with the intention that they will learn to read rather than in response to or with their buy-in, you have decentred your child and centred the thing you are doing.

I know of children who as soon as they could crawl, they moved away from being read to. As soon as a book came out to read to a sibling, that child disappeared from the room. They could have been forced to be read to (because being read to makes learning to read easier, right?), they could have been encouraged to play word games like 'I spy' or shamed for not wanting to play, they could have been forced to choose 'just two books' from the library every time (rather than refusing to choose any), they could have been left to figure out for themself what the game wanted them to do rather than having someone read the information to them.

These things decentre the child and centre the objective, in this case, learning to read.

Being the attentive adult means being attentive to the child you have and what they are telling you they do and do not need. Children learn to read in their own way and in their own time. Listening and responding to the child you have is a key aspect of unschooling and is no different when it comes to learning to read. Figure 8.1 shows how even the ingredients that enable learning to read without school are not a set of instructions, but are connected and responsive to your child.

D is for developmentally ready

Children learn when they are developmentally ready and able. There are so many things that need to be in place cognitively before reading, as we know it, can happen. There is a point where someone is able to read, and before that point they can't. No number of interventions or reading programmes will change that. They will change how your child feels about reading though.

Reading is also part of your child's developing skills in literacy. There is an interconnection between reading, writing, speaking and listening. Developmentally they progress in conjunction with one another. They are held together by the thread of communication. Learning to read isn't solely about assigning meaning to written words and understanding that meaning. Before your child learns to read, and as they continue to learn to develop their reading skills, they will also be acquiring the skills they need for writing and speaking and listening. This means that every conversation you have, every song you sing together, every TV show you watch, every social interaction you or they have with another person is also contributing to your child grasping reading when they are developmentally ready. It is one of the reasons why children and young people who learn to read later than their peers 'catch up' quickly as they frequently have a broader vocabulary to draw on because of their life experience and exposure as compared to younger children.

Susan notes how her understanding of her youngest child's development and child-centred approach helped her to know what her son needed and when:

> " I have always passionately believed that my children will learn something when they need something, or when it's useful to them, when it's relevant to their lives, or when they're interested in something. And reading very much fell into this, in terms of, gaming is his big passion, and in order to do well in the video game and to understand what's happening, and to properly immerse yourself in it, you often need to read the text that is there on the screen. And so, I would often read to him, *Fortnite* was a massive phase for a while so every day he would ask me 'What are the challenges today?' and I would read them.
>
> It suddenly occurred to me that he hadn't asked me what the daily challenge was, so I asked him, 'How are the challenges going today?' and he was like, 'I've done them'. 'How did you know what to do?' 'I read it.'

One day he said to me, 'I know my new water bottle will keep my water cold for 24 hours but only hot for 6', and I asked, 'How do you know that?' 'Well, I read it off the package.'

We never had any explicit teaching but gradually, over the years, I became aware that he was connecting more and more words together, in terms of their meaning and in their written form.

Being developmentally ready isn't something you can rush, but being aware of its necessity can equip you to confidently allow learning to read to unfold gently for your child.

E is for environment (filled with literacy)

We live in a literate-rich environment. We are immersed in language. Once we begin to see that 'reading' is not only about reading a story, loving books or the primary way of becoming educated, we can begin to see how words are everywhere. When we see words and reading everywhere, we can see how our children can access and learn to read in many ways, not purely through story books. Access to reading is unavoidable in our culture.

LITERACY IS EVERYWHERE

Let's take a moment together to look around the space that you're in and to spot any written words you can:

- A stack of fiction books in the corner
- A craft kit on the shelf
- A card from a friend
- The days of the week on a pair of socks
- Words carved into coasters
- Slogans on mugs and clothing
- The book you are reading
- Emails and messages on your phone.

The list goes on. And when you move from this comfy spot, more words surround you in every new place that you find yourself in.

> Take your time to walk around your house and notice any written words in each room, even the bathroom!
>
> Next, when you leave the house, continue to notice and see – what written words are there out there?

Reading is more than enjoying a good story book. It is the ability to see written language, to understand that those specific marks carry meaning, and to make sense of those marks and their meaning. It is more than being able to decipher what a word says; it is also how to interpret it. It can be as simple as reading the word 'pull' on a door and knowing that this is an instruction and what to do to be able to open the door. It's understanding what an author means when they use a phrase like, 'Mr Norris was an eye-smiler' or 'You can use the Cloak of Billowing as a bonus action'. It's more than just words. It's deciphering words and attaching them to meaning.

When we take the idea of reading books off its pedestal and see that words are everywhere, we can begin to trust the process. Your child is immersed in a life of literacy, with words flowing through our day-to-day living: talking, singing, discussing, writing, listening and communicating with and to each other. All these things contribute to your child being able to read.

Making sense of it all

Thousands of unschooled and self-directed young people have learned to read this way, and I have seen at least 20 of them do it with my own eyes. Children who learned to read when they were 12 or older. Children who are dyslexic. Children who had negative reading experiences at school. Children who have never been to school.

Parents worry more about whether they can *teach* their child to read than anything else. It has this elevated status along with writing and maths that somehow makes you feel like you need special skills to be able to do it. Or is it that it is seen as the gateway to all learning? If you can read, then you can learn anything. Either way, it is feared and revered with equal status.

The truth is that you don't need any teaching skill, a specific reading scheme or approach. You don't need to teach your child to read any more than you teach them the names of the dinosaurs or how to make their lunch. Your child will learn to read, and you will be there to facilitate that in the ways that they need. And until the point when they can do it by themself, you will also be there to read anything for them, so the gateway to learning via reading is always open.

It's not always easy. Not when schooled children are being taught to read at the age of four or five and your child might not read independently until they are in their adolescent years. And not when the process can look very different for different children. Our aim is not solely for our children to be able to read; what we want is for our children to have a positive experience with reading in whatever form that takes for them.

Susan remembers:

> “The manga light novels are in the last year. And he has been out of school for six-and-a-half years. I think this is one of the things when you're doing something that's not looking like school is holding the faith in the fact that you are creating that environment, and you're saying 'yes' to their passions, and surrounding them with literature, whatever form that takes, whether it be subtitles, whether it be reviews or whatever, and so it took five-and-a-half years of trusting that process.

The ABCs of learning to read in the real world are essentially the same principles for learning anything. The interaction between these five elements is symbiotic. You cannot sit down and teach these elements to your child. What you can do is cultivate a life that nurtures their intrinsic motivation and, most importantly, strengthens the adult–child relationship. In this way you are giving your child the gift of confidence and worth in their own abilities and self. This is trusting the process. How you interact with your child affects their view of reading and how they feel about themself as a reader. This is the biggest determinator of your child's relationship with their ability to learn to read. You cannot speed up the process, but you can make the path ahead smooth and pleasant.

Principles to live by

- Meeting current needs meets future needs.
- Relationship comes first.
- Personal drive enables learning.
- Children learn when they are developmentally ready and able.

Chapter 9

What to Expect as Unschooled Children Grow

Unschooled children are different. Their experience of the world is different, their relationships with family, friends and their community are different, the way they live is different, and how they learn is different. Throughout this book I have talked about how school does things and the effect that this can have on our children. I have also talked about how unschooling families approach things and the impact those choices have on our children. As our children grow up the difference between schooled and unschooled children becomes noticeably bigger and increasingly more obvious, especially for those in the habit of comparing their children with their schooled peers (which I don't recommend).

The truth is that schooled children often appear to be doing 'better', 'learning more' and getting on in life or growing up faster than children who are unschooled. That is, if you are holding them to the same outcomes and the same standards. Let's remember that growing up faster is a myth. It is defined by an arbitrary finish line and enforced expectations such as exam results or set career qualifications and goals. It doesn't necessarily mean 'better' and isn't achievable for everyone (schooled or otherwise). Children who are developing according to their own timeline play longer, accept support from others for longer (by which I mean that adults are needed to do more for and with their children), are more relaxed about the need to take exams and are often clearer about what *they* want to do and how *they* want to do it.

Children who are self-directed do grow and change, but as with most things, when we allow this to happen naturally it looks different to when children are moved along a prescribed route. Many parents ask me questions about when and how this happens. When will they read themselves? When will they do a workbook or some project work? When will they sleep in their own bed? When will they make their own lunch? When will they take an exam? We are so used to making children do these things that we have no marker for what happens when we don't arbitrarily make them do it. And when we do support the natural progression of learning, and every child has their own unique timeline, it can sometimes look like these things may never happen, especially when your child is last to read, never expresses interest in a project and you are still co-sleeping when they are 12 years old. The reality is that it is entirely possible that some of those things may never happen. Being okay with that and seeing the value in their own choices is crucial.

As you read this chapter it would be a good idea to keep these things in mind, that while I talk about stages, I am not presenting a step-by-step programme, that one day your child wakes up and is now experiencing a completely different stage. Learning and growing are not sequential and things ebb and flow. One day you witness a glimmer of change, a new thing achieved, and then the next day they revert to where they were before, and that new thing isn't seen again for months or years. In the same way that learning belongs to the learner, we can never be sure how the experiences that our children are having are contributing to their growth and development, we can never be sure what leap or change is happening now or next.

The stages I talk about here are taken from observations of many unschooled young people over many years, from reflecting on their past years. They are not a programme of development to be used as a guide to push our children into, and nor will all children and young people experience all the indicators in each stage. They will always be growing and developing, and no one can write a predicted account and timed path for them. Your child will progress in their own time and in their own way – remember that not much stays the same forever.

The schooled path

Culturally, the first 18 years of your child's life is largely mapped out for them, and rather shockingly, it isn't that much different to the first 18 years of your own life. There may be a few variations, but broadly speaking the same things will happen at the same time: your child is registered at a school by the age of four and being taught to read within the first few weeks; in Year 1 your child is expected to spend the vast majority of their day sat at a table doing work that has been set by a teacher; in Year 2 they will learn about the Great Fire of London and take their SATs; at the end of primary school Year 6 will take a residential trip together; the following school year your child will move to secondary school. Somewhere in the next few years they will possibly go on a foreign exchange trip and narrow down their subject choices, and by Year 10 they will be studying for their GCSEs, ready to sit them in the summer of Year 11. Then comes work experience. This is usually followed by a further two years in education where they are expected to have chosen subjects or training for their future careers.

I once sat in a parent-teacher meeting, as the teacher, and was asked by the parents if I thought their child would go to Oxbridge. The child was four years old and had been at school for a little over six weeks. The end goal had been set, the next 12 years of her life would be dominated by this expectation and her future defined for her. Between school and her parents, the path ahead was clear and well defined. With this in mind, every step of her childhood can be broken down into increments and geared towards this target. There is little active involvement from the child in the decisions being made or whether it is a developmentally appropriate approach. This is maybe an extreme case, but it is how the school system works for every child. It is a one-size-fits-all system with a clear end goal.

Schools don't just map out academic learning; they introduce and impose other requirements on children too. Being separated from their main carer at the age of four, being expected to dress and undress themselves for PE class from Reception, sitting for extended periods of time, asking permission to go to the toilet, being outside at playtime with large numbers of unknown children, having no contact with parents on the school residential and being away from home for a week, navigating travelling on their own to secondary school, making choices about their future in their teen years – there is a strong culture of growing independence by forcing independence. There is little consideration for the individual and a disregard for genuinely involving young people.

As parents we carry these ideas with us into our unschooling life. We often continue to hold these benchmarks in our minds and panic a little when our children don't, or are unable to, do those things. We worry that they may never leave our side, go to a group without us, play at a friend's house without us staying, sleep in their own bed all night (or at all) or decide what they want to do for a job. The path that is so clearly set before them in school, with streetlights at key junctions, signposts in all the right places, directions called out like a sat nav, and an end destination already decided, just doesn't exist in the same way.

The unschooling path can feel more like a trip into the wilderness. The path is unclear and overgrown with brambles, weeds and overhanging plants. The light is often dappled through the dense foliage and can be so dark in places that it is difficult to see any way forward. There are fewer people on the same trip as you and there are regular feelings of uncertainty. It feels this way because it is outside our experience and the societal norm, but it can also feel amazing once we are able to relax into what we are doing and see the wonderful life that our child is leading and the way in which they become increasingly independent when they are ready.

Seasons of unschooling

As we move away from a standardised view of child development and embrace the vast differences and diversity among human beings, it is still possible to observe and outline different seasons of unschooling. It is impossible to ignore that **your child will change, develop and grow in their own time**, even if these happen at a broad range of ages, in individual pathways, and in unique ways.

Figure 9.1 attempts to demonstrate how children change, develop and grow naturally, because they do manage it without schooled techniques. It's hard to do though because so much of the modern research that we have is impacted by centuries of schooling and because, from my observations, there is no one set of sequential milestones or set age markers. This is why I have chosen to use the term 'season' and illustrate it with a curved line, to represent movement and flow from one to another and back again.

It is also essential to remember that throughout their lives and all the seasons they pass through, the most important thing is always their relationship with you. Your deep and secure **connection is key** and always comes first.

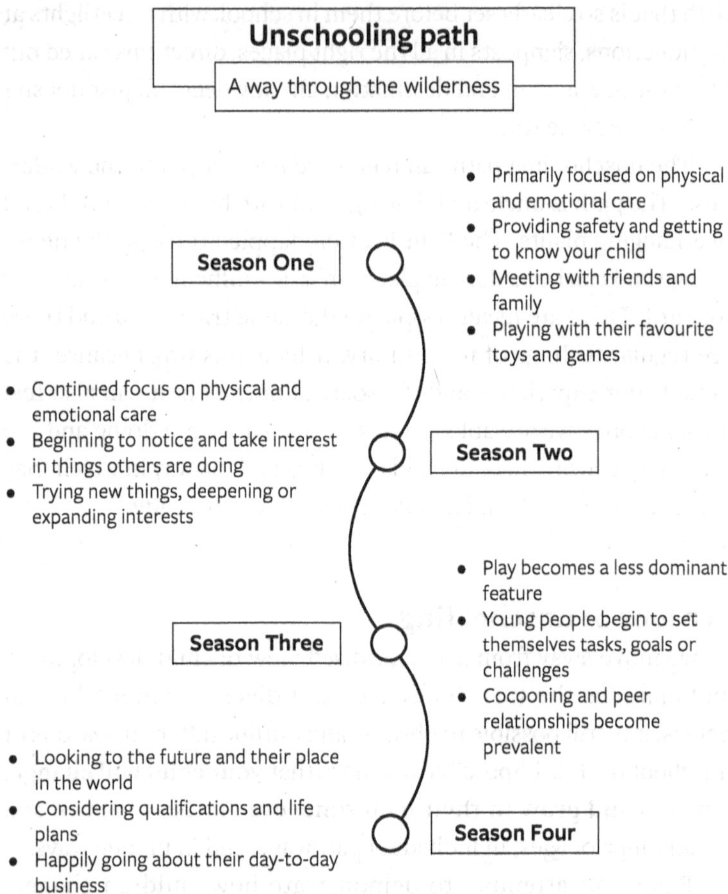

Figure 9.1. *The unschooling path*

Season One

Your child will be most likely be growing and changing at an enormous visible rate. They will highly likely enjoy exploring the world through all their senses. Touch, taste, smells, holding/stroking/rubbing everything. This is the time when their learning will look mostly like the play we are familiar with. They will naturally want to be by your side a lot of the time and want to be involved in the things you are doing. They may well move quickly between one activity and another and need a lot of guidance and support with social interactions and emotional literacy.

As parents this is an intense few years as our children's physical and emotional needs are high, and your supervision, presence, guidance and help are constantly required and there isn't much time for keeping the house in order or for yourself. However, you can relax about the idea of pulling them away from the things they are loving, like playing in the bath, painting and playing with pots and pans, because you can be confident that they are learning through their play and real-life experiences. You also have more opportunity to lean into their need to sleep during the day, eat constantly and embrace the need for a lot of movement during their waking hours.

Sorrel described how things were for their eldest at this stage:

> "My son's proximity to me and his physical contact with me has been really, really, really, really, really important. I was glued to the sofa, just cuddling him. I spent so much time doing that. What was needed from me is mental and emotional availability, and what that requires is for me to really look after myself and enjoy those moments of calm, because they don't always last. Creating capacity within myself so that, if my son does want to list all of the dragons in *Dragon City* to me, I can be there and listen and not be desperate to get away.

This is an intensive season and I want to write with assurance that this passes, but the reality is that it may not pass so easily for some. The beauty of unschooling is that you can be fully present for as long as your child needs you to be.

This is the time to have a variety of different resources available within your home, and to have tables or baskets preprepared with various items or crafts readily set up for your child. They may not get used, and that's okay. It serves a dual purpose, though, as children can visibly see what is on offer, like an invitation to play, and it can make a moment easier for you if everything is already set up. It is also completely okay to respond to your child's ideas if they pull out something else instead.

It is also during this period of time that you may notice how your child is drawn to certain activities or toys. Anyone with more than one child will marvel at how different they are, even during these young years. One child regularly plays with cars and constantly wants to watch the trains go by from the local bridge. Another child chooses to sit in the dirt, and fills their pockets with sticks and stones. You might have craft materials available that have hardly been touched for years before child number three comes along and uses the whole supply in a matter of weeks.

Getting to know your child in all ways is an essential part of their unschooling journey. As you spend your days together you will be learning about what makes them tick, what and how they like to play, places they feel most relaxed in, tuning into their eat/sleep and play rhythms.

Now is also the time to connect with other local home educators at flexible social meets in parks, playgrounds, woods and beaches, or stay-and-play events. In fact, I highly recommend it. Even if your child isn't feeling sociable you can connect with local families online or go to spaces where they are meeting, even if your child only has eyes for you. It will be beneficial for you to have a support network.

Season Two

This is a season of children testing things out, giving things a go, spreading their wings and seeing what there is out there. Children become increasingly aware of things outside the home that are on offer to them. Maybe their friend is in a home ed gymnastics class, or they see a ballet dancer on YouTube, or a film advertised at the cinema. They can become quite keen to do all the things, asking simultaneously if they can paint a picture, go swimming, have their hair braided and go to their friend's house to play. Remember, though, that not every class will suit them; they may still need help to get the paints out and enjoy you sitting with them and painting too; swimming might not mean swimming lessons; it is possible they may want to try braiding their own hair but still need you to do it for them in the end; and you may need to go to the friend's house too. During this season, even though they are stepping out a little and discovering more, they will most likely still need you close by and on hand.

Remember that every child is different. Some children won't

ever be interested in classes and them joining in or trying out their options may lead back to them doing things that look completely different to what you are familiar with. They may never even try a class. Who they are and how they choose to do things will come into sharper focus, though. Providing spaces for them that fuels their fire – whether that is making cosy dens at home or making contact with friends every day, watching box sets of their favourite show or exposing them to new art supplies regularly – is equally important.

As parents we may become involved in organising different experiences and trips outside the home, opening up our home to friends for play dates, and researching subscriptions, TV shows and nearby specialists for a whole range of different interests. Some of you may have children who continue to need you to be constantly by their side and rely on your local home ed community to organise get-togethers, clubs or trips that you can join in, and that's okay too.

Many children continue to play in the fashion that we are familiar with (while their schooled peers have predominantly left this behind them now). Their learning may be less obvious and not as rapid, and commonly this is when parents notice the ever-growing gap between what their child is doing compared to their schooled peers. Hang on in there, look for the engagement and passion, and continue to enjoy your time with your child as they happily participate in the world around them on their own terms.

This exercise is helpful when you come to think about the changes that are happening, the progress that is being made and reflecting on how your child is developing, growing and learning in their own time. It does come with a warning: this is not an assessment tool and shouldn't be used as such. It can be employed to calm any rising worries about whether or how your child is progressing.

PROGRESS REVIEW

This is an exercise in two parts – the first part for you to consider now, and the second part for you to come back to in three to six months' time. Set a reminder for yourself so that there is a chance that you will remember to do it. Put a note on there of the chapter and page number too. Alternatively, you can do it retrospectively. Complete the first part as if it were a year ago (or three to six months ago) and the second part as of today.

So often when we are with our children day in day out we cannot see the small micro changes that are happening right before our eyes. Looking at the same thing and reflecting on it after a significant amount of time can identify and reassure us of the things that are progressing and the skills they are developing.

Part One

Make notes for a few days of the things your child is doing and any skills they are using.

- How do they spend their time?
- What questions are they asking?
- What activities/toys are their favourite?
- How do they play with others?
- What places do they like going to?
- What can they do?

Also list other things that you notice.

Part Two: Reflect

Part Two should be done a significant interval after Part One. Suggested periods of time are three, six or twelve months later.

Reflect directly on your previous observations and on the skills you listed and how they have progressed since you wrote them here.

Part Two: Review

Review what your child is doing by considering the same questions afresh. Make notes for a few days of the things your child is doing.

- How do they spend their time?
- What questions are they asking?

- What activities/toys are their favourite?
- How do they play with others?
- What places do they like going to?
- What can they do?

Also list other things that you notice.

Season Three

As a child approaches or grows into adolescence, they can often experience a period of cocooning. Where once we had a child who would not be comfortable with us leaving the room, now they won't leave theirs! It can be difficult for us to know exactly what they are doing all the time in comparison to when they were younger. However, when we do catch a glimpse at what they are spending their time doing, we often see a shift in how they now approach their learning. There is often less purely playful moments, and increasingly our young people will find a goal that they are trying to achieve. It might be completing the level on a video game, it could be building a complex LEGO® Technic™ set, it might be mastering the drawing of a horse, or spending hours finding out about marine life. It feels more like they have set themselves a target, a goal or a project even if it's something small, like finding out about guinea pigs or making it to the top of the climbing wall.

It can sometimes appear that our young person no longer needs us as they enter this season, but appearances can be deceiving. What they need from us changes from what has gone before. You may find yourself with pockets of time to pursue your own interests or spend some time on yourself. This is the period when we need to be increasingly purposeful about seeking out connection with our young people, weaving in time together, opportunities to chat, and responding warmly when they seek us out. We need to be ready and willing to engage and respond to them on their terms: **be attentive and available for your child.**

May Ling talked about some of the differences she sees now that her two daughters are aged 11 and 9:

> There's that element when they were younger, I feel like a lot of the hard work has been done: always listening to them when they have something to say; always inviting them to share what they're experiencing; giving them words to help them express what they're saying, what they're trying to say; helping them in their relationships, but always in a consensual way. Your role as the parent is always changing, depending on the situation, how much they want to do it themselves, and how much they would like you to lead them a bit, and how it's different for each child, because they are different.

Parents can practically help to find mentors, classes, books and events that are specifically related to the passions their child has. Offer them opportunities to expand on the skills and interests they have. Continue to ensure that the equipment they need is freely available to them and repair, replace and upgrade their resources as necessary. Be available for them to bounce their ideas off on you or info dump their latest focus. Be prepared to drive them to locations and meet-ups or travel with them on public transport. Support them as they need, continuing to prioritise your relationship with them, and accepting them right where they are. Each young person will continue to need individualised support with their interests, approach to learning and needs, and that's okay.

Season Four

As our young people move into young adulthood they begin to be focused on future goals and how to achieve them. This may include qualifications, apprenticeships, volunteering, setting up their own business, applying to university or another path that they create for themselves as they venture into adulthood. They continue to be at liberty to confidently try things out, make mistakes, change direction, be happy with their day-to-day or invest fully in their dreams. There is no one given outcome, no one set of acceptable standards or a pass mark.

May Ling shared an account of a young person who came out of school during their teen years:

> “I know a child who only came out of school two years ago, he was 14, and in that time, him and his mum, and therefore his family, went through a rapid adjustment process. She had bought into the school system until that point, but his mental health was seriously declining, and he wanted to come out of school. In that time, he was cocooning, and it was enough for him to be to be allowed that decision, to be allowed to leave, to then figure out who he is and what he wants to do. He's decided to join a college, and he's decided to do certain courses, and he's managing his own schedule, and is very much developing his confidence as a 16-year-old, and really finding himself.

This season can occur beyond the legal age of schooling, but as parents, we continue to support our children as we have done all the while, as much as they want, and in ways that they need. In the book *Inventing Ourselves: The Secret Life of the Teenage Brain* by Sarah-Jayne Blakemore she talks about how the brain isn't fully configured until humans reach their mid-20s. Children and young people who have been following their natural developmental pathways and not forced into making career plans and life choices in their teenage years may take their time to do so. The joy of unschooling is that it doesn't adhere to an arbitrary timeline and that there is no sense of time lost or being left behind when we understand that anyone can learn anything that they want or need to at the time they need to know it.

Conversely, your young adult may have taken exams, launched their own business or been involved in volunteering or community work that aligns with their passions long before they turn 18. It isn't just the gap between schooled and unschooled young people that widens; we also see a wide variety of life choices being made among unschooled young people, because when children are given the space to make their own choices we find that humans come up with a huge variety of ways in which to go about living. **Learning never ends, and there is no definitive end point.**

The possibilities for our young people are not hindered by their education. In fact, it can be argued that their life and learning pathway equips them better for their adulthood. I have met several unschooled adults and follow others on social media. I have met librarians, tech consultants, those who work in the media, artists and more. Important, though, is the fact that these adults are happy with the education and upbringing that they experienced, and are happy with the life they now lead. Most disappear happily into their adult lives without a trace.

In 2015 Peter Gray and Gina Riley conducted research on grown unschoolers' evaluations of their unschooling experiences, and an overwhelming number of participants expressed high satisfaction with their unschooling experience.[1] They valued the freedom it provided to follow their interests in a manner that suited them best. They recognised how unschooling enhanced their self-motivation, self-guidance, accountability and lifelong learning abilities. A small number of respondents mentioned facing a learning gap due to unschooling, yet they were generally successful in overcoming it when necessary. The majority expressed contentment with their social lives during unschooling, highlighting the benefits of forming friendships across diverse age groups. Only three respondents reported unhappiness with their unschooling experience, attributing it to social seclusion and dysfunctional family dynamics involving psychologically depressed and uninvolved parents.

Expect the unexpected

As with all things outside the standardised system, it is not black and white, and children do not progress through one season to the next overnight. It is not clear-cut like a birthday, when yesterday you were eight and today you are nine. There is no line in the sand they cross over and never return to how things were before. The skills that categorise each season develop, rehearse, and are mastered slowly over time, and not all the characteristics of one season will show themselves all at the same time. But over large periods of time we can observe these changes and see how things naturally progress. It might be that one day in one moment you recognise that

1 Gray, Peter and Riley, Gina (2015) *Grown Unschoolers' Evaluations of Their Unschooling Experiences: Report I on a Survey of 75 Unschooled Adults.* CUNY Academic Works. https://academicworks.cuny.edu/hc_pubs/480

they did something differently, they tried a new approach, advocated for themselves or made a suggestion where before they always needed guiding. Just a flicker. Like when they say they might sleep in their own bed tonight. It also might be a further two years before they do. Small changes and micro steps happen all the time, often undetected. It isn't until we reflect and remember that we see how things have changed.

Humans are complex, and the way that society has categorised children into standardised boxes has altered how we view childhood and our expectations. When we live outside of that box it is harder to grasp something tangible. As we centre our child it isn't as simple as saying, 'This target has been reached' or 'They have achieved their goal' just because they did something once. It isn't solely about what they can do; it is also about how they feel towards it and the different scenarios they are comfortable using it in. There are so many different factors involved. Your young person is unique and their unschooling journey will be as unique as they are.

Essentially, the truth is that your child is always growing, creating an understanding of the world around them, developing an understanding of themself, acquiring new knowledge and skills. They are doing it in their own unique way, in their own unique timing, but it is happening. There is no one map or path that everyone will follow. Expect to be surprised, and **expect the unexpected**.

Principles to live by

- Your child will change, develop and grow in their own time.
- Connection is key.
- Be attentive and available for your child.
- Learning never ends, and there is no definitive end point.
- Expect the unexpected.

Chapter 10

The One Thing that You Need

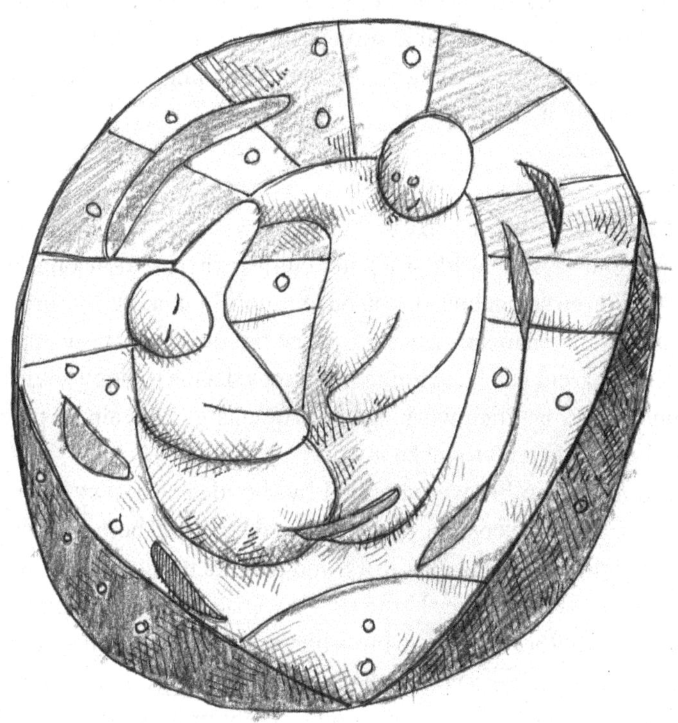

What is the one thing that you need to be able to unschool? 'One thing?', you say. How can it be possible that you only need one thing to be able to unschool? I can think of five things right now.

It's not that you don't need other things too. This one thing, though, is the biggest part of the unschooling picture, and it is often the part that is overlooked. Parents worry about academics, exams and progression. They worry about scheduling and putting in structure and timetables and having a plan. They worry about socialisation and screen time – all of which have been talked about from an unschooling perspective in the pages of this book.

There is also one thing that has been mentioned like a thread through all of it. And now it is time for that one thing to have a chapter all to itself! Because without it, all the other changes and adjustments that you make might not quite hit the mark, but with it all those other things will fall beautifully into place.

Let's start by asking families who are actively unschooling what they think. I took an informal survey and asked families, 'What is the one thing that you need when you are unschooling?' Unsurprisingly, I got a range of answers.

Money, money, money

Money is always a consideration in a culture where two-income families are often struggling, or you have simply built a lifestyle around your current financial situation. Some families lose an income so that one parent can be at home when they decide to home educate; others rearrange their working hours or change jobs; single-parent families juggle it all to make it work.

Families can be overwhelmed by the idea that they are now financially responsible for their child's education. There is no available funding for home educators, and parents take on full financial responsibility when they home educate. It seems to be a point that many local authorities like to press home and can raise concerns over whether you can unschool well on a limited budget. Maybe you are on benefits, or down to a one-income family, or have other financial restrictions. Maybe you are acutely aware that you don't have the money to invest in a lot of resources, big days out or classes.

From the (informal) survey that I did, finances are a serious consideration. It takes a considerable amount of creative thinking and reconsideration of priorities to find a way forward. The good news is, you can unschool and unschool well whatever your income. Creating a full, interesting and engaging life is fully accessible without large amounts of expendable cash.

Finding time for 'me time'

A significant number of responses talked about the importance of parents taking care of themselves – whether that was ensuring they had enough sleep, accessing therapies, moments of silence, regular walks in nature, other adult friends or coffee!

When you are taking care of your children 24/7 there is no respite. Many of us have children who have high attachment needs and there is no opportunity for traditional 'me time'. This doesn't mean that we shouldn't find ways in which to take care of ourselves. Start by asking yourself what it is that you really need, and then consider what 1 per cent of that would look like (see Table 10.1).

Table 10.1. Finding time for 'me time'

What I need:	What that looks like as 1%:
Lots of sleep	Having blankets readily available so that I can curl up on the sofa, and quieter activities – e.g. LEGO, colouring, audio books and cartoons – that the children can do without me, alongside a tray of snacks!
Moments of silence	Safely leaving the children to play and taking 5 minutes sat on the back doorstep; investing in ear plugs or noise-reducing headphones
Regular walks in nature	Taking my shoes off and putting my feet in the grass at the play park, joining the children in a river paddle, or cloud watching from the window
Adult friendship and community	Connecting with the real-life local community and finding unschooling families and groups online
Coffee (anyone who knows me knows that I am a tea drinker, so this information applies to all hot beverages!)	Investing in beautiful microwavable mugs (to make you smile and reheat your drink that has gone cold!). Treat yourself to high quality coffee for when you have a moment to really enjoy it

Keeping you in the picture is important. It is one of the top reasons that folk give up unschooling as parents apply regular expectations and solutions to the concept of 'me time' and fall short of taking care of themselves. Recognising your own needs and meeting them with compassion and care is important. It is highly likely that it won't be perfect, but don't ignore yourself altogether – you are an essential element in your family, so take care of you.

Prioritising relationships

Overwhelmingly the responses from the survey were all things associated with building strong relationships with our children. Participants named aspects such as: time, connection, patience, flexibility, autonomy, understanding, fun, respect, trust and truly listening.

I had a fantastic conversation with Nici when I interviewed her. She has been unschooling for over 10 years and has four children. Three of them attended school, but when her third child was seriously undersupported, they took the decision to deregister and the other two quickly followed. Her fourth child has never been to school and is a lifelong unschooler. She has a wealth of knowledge and experience that she uses to help and support home ed families. We discussed the things that people think they need and focus on when setting out to home educate – the money, the space, the educational resources – and I asked her, 'What do you think is the one thing that families really need in order to be able to unschool well?'

Her answer was spot on!

> “ You need presence. That's literally what you need. It's not even about time, because having free time does not mean that you're present in your children's lives. Being around at the same time as your children doesn't mean you're present with them. So, I think for me, it doesn't matter what you've got. It doesn't matter whether you've got 100 different resources to be able to strew around the house if you don't have any idea what your children are engaging with and what they're not; what they're enjoying and what they're not; what they're feeling.

> The only way that we can know any of those things is to be present in their lives.

Unschooling as a philosophy considers how children learn; in practice it is primarily focused on how children feel. Learning happens and happens well when they are comfortable and confident where they are and with the people they are with. The more relaxed, content and happy they are, the greater capacity they have to consider new ideas and explore new ways. Feeling safe, loved and accepted changes how a child views the world and interacts with it, and this improves the quality of their learning. The relationship with your child becomes the main priority in unschooling; it is the one thing that will have the biggest impact on your unschooling life.

Centring your child, building a strong and connected relationship with them, supercharges all the practical efforts that you are making. It enables you to tailor your efforts to your child, optimising the experience based on your deep knowledge and understanding of who they are as a person. It requires you first and foremost to know your child, to know them well, and to love and accept them just the way they are.

The power of compassion

Compassion is the cornerstone of rebuilding relationships with our children. It involves understanding, empathy and a genuine desire to **see your child for who they are**, and acknowledge and meet the needs they have. When we approach our children with compassion, we create a safe and nurturing environment that fosters trust and mutual respect.

Children, like adults, have their own emotions, fears and challenges. By acknowledging their feelings and validating their experiences, we show them that their emotions are important and that they are not alone, and through co-regulation we can help them to navigate and process those thoughts and feelings. Seeing the world from our child's perspective builds a strong emotional bond and helps children feel understood and valued.

Approaching our child with compassion allows us to recognise that they are still learning and growing in developmentally appropriate ways. It helps us to respond to their behaviours with patience and kindness. This strengthens our relationship with them as we establish ourselves as their partner, advocating for them and being by their side, even in the stormy parts.

Compassion encourages open communication. When children feel safe and understood, they are more likely to express their thoughts and feelings openly. This is why children often act differently at home or around their main caregiver. This is where they feel safest and can honestly share how they are feeling. Building strong relationships means recognising that this is indicative of a good thing. Beginning with compassion is the first step to building relationships where you can work together with open and honest communication.

Compassion isn't only for the stormy moments, though. When we know our child well, we can begin to pre-empt needs and bring joy to our interactions with them on their own terms. We can show them love and affection in ways that are meaningful to them. We can recognise the time and conditions needed for them to feel calm, relaxed, engaged and curious, and to thrive. Compassion enables us to see who our child is and what they need to engage with the world in meaningful ways, and then provide it with grace and abundance.

Lastly, compassion fosters a sense of security and belonging. When children know that they are loved unconditionally, they feel more confident and secure in their relationship with us. This sense of security is vital for their emotional development and, in the long term, helps them navigate the world with resilience and self-assurance.

Compassion is essential for rebuilding relationships with our children. It allows us to connect on a deeper level, respond with empathy, encourage open communication and create a secure and loving environment. By embracing compassion, we can strengthen our bond with our children and support their emotional growth and wellbeing. It is the first step not only in building a strong relationship but also in re-establishing parent–child dynamics.

Figure 10.1 shows how the core components of compassion, connection and collaboration work together as the foundations for building strong relationships and establishing or improving family equity.

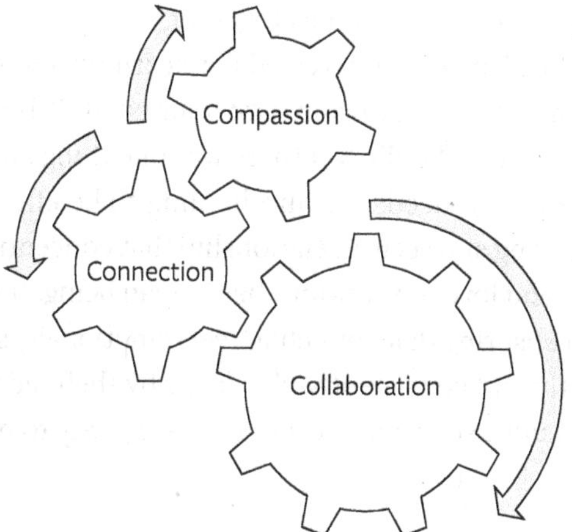

Figure 10.1. *Building relationships*

The need for connection

So many families have followed advice from experts that encouraged strict schedules for their newborns: leaving babies to 'cry it out'; attending nursery from a young age; tracking their developmental milestones; attending school full time by the age of four. As families, we live separate lives – adults in the workplace or home, and children at school. If you are fortunate, your schedules all work together in sync and you can see each other in the evenings or at weekends. Even then, these times are often occupied with homework or activities and clubs for the children. Families are ushered into a state of disconnection.

For your child this means that the core relationship they build with you is often impacted by the lack of time they have truly spent with you. The relationship becomes perfunctory. It is largely based on the routines you have in place in order to get your child to school on time, make sure that they have clean clothes and the right kit for the day, ensuring that homework is done, that they go to bed on time, that they have the right hairstyle, and have everything ready for the fete/swim meet/outing/test that is coming up. A large proportion of your time with your child is orchestrated around the requirements from things outside your home. There is little time left to be together or to do things together.

Unschooling isn't only interested in relearning how to learn but also rebuilding your relationship with your child. It is a key factor in the success of unschooling. If there was one thing and one thing only that your child needs for unschooling to be effective, it is a connected, strong and secure relationship that concentrates on the nurture, care and love towards another human being. It is primarily interested in ensuring that your child feels emotionally safe and has you constantly and consistently physically by their side, as well as on their side, until such a point that they are ready to move away.

Getting to know you

Spending so much time together can feel like foreign ground. It requires getting to know your child while your child is also getting to know themself. It requires space and time and the ability for adults to simply observe, to really see what it is that lights your child's fire and what it is that makes them feel loved, to think about what your child needs, and not what others tell you your child needs. It looks beyond what they are doing, what their interests are and what they are learning. If bed sharing helps them to sleep peacefully, then consider how you can make that happen; if they need to eat little and often rather than three bigger meals a day, work out how to do that; if they need help getting dressed when their friends can all do it themselves, keep helping them until they can do it themself; if they hate stories but love a particular gaming app, play the game with them and ditch the stories.

This is how we, as humans, including children, are heard. When we say this is how we like a thing, or this is our favourite colour, or I need to sleep, or I need to read this book again (for the 365th time) and the person they are with says, 'YES! You can do that, let me help you, let's do that thing together, I can make that possible for you', it makes a difference. To be truly seen by someone else. For them to notice you beyond the routines and 'have to do' and 'should be doing' of the day. To have your joys, sorrows, passions, and pains, likes, dislikes and needs acknowledged. This is to say to your child, 'I hear you'.

To do this we must be prepared to put aside our expectations and schedules, and prioritise our relationship with our child. Pause a moment and recognise that they are in the room. Notice the impact that a decision, activity or situation is truly having on them, and see the impact that life is having on the relationship you have and the way they think about themself.

Simply enjoying being together

The act of taking an interest in what your child is doing and being fully present while they talk about, show you or share with you what they are doing is a simple yet powerful way to acknowledge them. Connecting with them can be empathising with how they are feeling and truly seeking to understand their experience. For many parents, in those first few months it can be creating regular and predictable touch points throughout the day: bringing food at set times and staying in your young person's presence a little longer each time. Or being present in the same room together, maybe not playing or chatting together, but simply being in the same space together. The important thing is to **enjoy your time together** and know in doing this you are purposefully and intentionally creating an environment in which learning will flourish.

It might be that you find things of common interest to do together and connect over shared experiences. Having conversations and sharing ideas over a film you have both watched or an app that you both use, even if you do that independently from each other. Visiting a gallery for the afternoon or going ice skating together or having lunch at a local café without the background noise of being there to learn something. Simply sink into the pleasure of being together.

People are more important than things

Like almost anything worth doing, repairing relationships takes time, and establishing a new dynamic can be a rocky process. Things won't change overnight. Building trust, respect and connection takes as long as it takes. The good news is that now your child is out of school, you have a lot of time together. Saying 'yes!' to your child is one way of connecting with them and rebalancing the dynamics between you. There are other things that will help too (see Table 10.2).

Table 10.2. Six ways to connect with your young person

1. Saying 'yes' to their ideas and the things they want to do
2. Sitting and listening to them without rushing off to complete your next task or job; being a witness to their life and what it is they need to share with you
3. Spending five minutes or more snuggling together first thing in the morning and last thing at night. (If you don't like snuggling, then don't do it! Five minutes lying in bed together or sitting on the sofa or sharing breakfast is the same thing. It's about slowing down and spending concentrated time together focused on a human being)
4. Go the extra mile. When your child asks you to pass them their cup that is on the opposite side of the room to you, but right next to them, do it with care
5. Add sparkle to your interactions. Put tomato sauce on their plate in the shape of a smiley face, add your own comment and edits to GIFs and memes you share, use the fairy tea set for lunch and have mini food, have a kitchen disco, let them face paint you
6. Join them in their games and activities (if they will let you) or take an active interest

The hardest work for us really is the unpicking of the narrative we have been handed – ideas that are embedded in our society, like, 'You're spoiling your child' or 'They won't be able to take directions and do what they're told', 'You need to show them who is in charge' and 'How is this educational?'

Nici shared how she first approached this when they began unschooling over 10 years ago and how it's going now:

> “For me, it was about really starting to understand what our principles, for our family, were going to be. That started with what a lot of people call a home ed charter. But for us, it started as rules for our household, and it definitely is not called that anymore. It is called a charter. We do all sign it, and we only agree to it once. All of us agree with absolutely everything that's on it. That wasn't the case when we first started home ed. I can remember the first one that we did. I felt I was so progressive, by going ‘We're all going to sit around the table and decide’. I didn't mean ‘We're all going to decide’. What I meant was, ‘I'm going to decide, and I'm going to judge by your reactions to things how much I need to convince you otherwise’. I can see that now, but at the time, I thought I was this amazing, therapeutic, very hippy approach, being very low demand and all of these kinds of things. And I was not doing any of those things, but I was a lot further on the journey than I had been previously.
>
> I remember one of those particular things that looks very different in our charter now compared to then. It said, ‘We will do as mummy says’, but it now says, ‘Everything is debatable’, everything! And the journey between ‘You do as I say’ to ‘Everything is debatable’ has been a 10-year journey. That doesn't mean that I'm quite there with ‘Everything is debatable’, because sometimes I really wish not everything was debatable, but it's that journey. I think for me the biggest thing was I came up with some principles that I felt were really, really important.

We often have an urge for things to change overnight and for there to be one grand answer. Rebuilding relationships takes time – time and effort every day, mostly in small consistent ways that often go unnoticed. It means intentionally slowing down, paying attention to the people right in front of us, and remembering that **people are more important than things**. It also takes the passage of time. Living outside the norm means that we are constantly faced with the challenge of unpicking things we have long held to be true, and this is as much true about our relationships and what parent–child dynamics should look like as it is about education, learning and child development.

The key is to keep making better choices, to keep prioritising your relationship and to do things that centre your young person so that they are seen, heard and understood.

Moving towards collaboration

Establishing a new relational dynamic with compassion and connection at the heart of our interactions with our children builds strong relationships. Over time, the mutual trust and respect we cultivate creates space for sharing opinions and guidance. This approach is not about control or coercion but rather provides parents with a platform to share experiences and knowledge. Most importantly, it offers young people a safe space to express their thoughts and opinions.

Drop the battles

You may have heard the phrase 'choose your battles'. Have you ever considered dropping the battles altogether? The norm of constant conflict with our children, where hierarchy must be established and absolute control maintained, undermines your child's sense of safety and self. It leaves them adrift in a stormy world without a co-pilot, fostering self-doubt and limiting their learning. It is entirely possible to live a life without battling with your child. This doesn't mean there won't be disagreements or challenges with some of your child's decisions, and nor does it mean you will always share the same opinions. Dropping the battles isn't about letting them do whatever they want, but it also isn't coercion by another name.

Dropping the battles requires us to reimagine how we interact with our children, when and how we guide and assist them, to seriously think about what is necessary, and adopting respectful and considerate ways to engage with your child that honour their personhood.

Working together

This is about collaboration and how we **work together in partnership**. It's about setting aside your fears and choosing a more peaceful path. It's about intentionally doing things together rather than adults doing things to children. It's about enabling your child to make meaningful choices in their day for themself in a safe and supported environment.

Building connection takes time. It takes more than a moment to wait for your child to be ready to brush their teeth or to help them make their own breakfast. It can take hours to focus on their emotions and needs rather than correcting behaviour. In our society, there often isn't time for that.

Not anymore. Now you have the gift of time. You can focus on your child and your relationship. You can come alongside them and take your time. Take your time to watch, listen and understand. You can focus on your child's experience and how they feel and respond rather than focusing on the task or the expectation. The focus isn't on the list of age-related tasks your child should know or be doing; the focus is on being with your child. It's not about whether they have completed a set of activities, but whether they have been active participants in their morning. Doing anything with enthusiasm and flow (or not doing them at all!) and them taking longer is far better than herding them through with pressure and stress.

You are now coming alongside your child and responding to them in ways that bring peace and ease. You are actively involving your child in their life. You are working together to find solutions, questioning the go-to answers and exploring new ways together. It becomes a much slower way to live because discovering needs and meeting them with compassion, acknowledging and honouring emotions and connecting with your child, and collaborating with them takes more time. This is how strong relationships are built. This is how we truly get to know each other, to know ourselves, and for your child to know and honour themself. They can grow in authentic ways, free from the shame and self-loathing brought on by constant expectations and directives they cannot or do not want to achieve or fulfil.

Collaboration in action

I once saw two unschooled friends, Fred (11) and William (12), sitting together, each on their own laptop, starting to play a new game they had found. They agreed to do the walkthrough tutorial before playing. The tutorial was text-based, and William, the older of the two, was not a fluent reader. Fred finished quickly and urged his friend to 'Hurry up'. William replied, 'I can't read as well as you; it's going to take me longer'. Imagine how this would have played out in a school setting. A 12-year-old who wasn't a fluent reader, hoping to join a game with friends that required keeping up with the text. William might have felt embarrassed or ashamed, and his friends might have grown tired of waiting, leaving him behind. None of that happened here. Fred simply asked, 'Would you like me to read it out for you?' and William accepted. A simple, everyday interaction, but when compared to what often happens elsewhere, something ordinary becomes extraordinary.

I observe the same when I see adolescents playing computer games together. Friends who know each other so well and know the games they play together so well that they understand who excels at which roles. They spend immense amounts of time playing team games that require in-depth knowledge of each other, the game and the characters they play. They tutor each other through different roles, giving friends the opportunity to improve and guiding them on how to play well. They decide whether to swap roles in a 'real game' against other teams or stick to their strengths. They cheer each other on, encourage each other, and occasionally lose their shit when things go unexpectedly well or badly. They see everyone's strengths and know how to work with them through collaboration.

It's not all sunshine and rainbows. They are human, after all. They get frustrated with each other and sometimes prefer to play with others who match their skill level. However, it's mostly handled with kindness, and when it isn't, they address it and repair their friendships through reconnection. It's messy, loud, stressful, argumentative and complex. By continually centring the people, relationships and friendships involved, collaboration becomes a well-practised habit.

None of this has been taught through formal programmes or lessons. They haven't role-played scenarios or analysed interactions to demonstrate how things could be done differently. These young people have lived through experiences of being treated with respect, listened to, accepted unconditionally and having relationships restored and repaired. Their lived experiences have equipped them with the skills and blueprint needed to live alongside others with respect, to support those who need it and honour their own needs. They have been provided with a framework for compassion, connection and collaboration that impacts how they interact with the world now and in the future, optimising their learning capabilities and shaping their future relationships and interactions.

The following exercise is a family audit in collaborative behaviours, a chance to take a fresh look at what is working well in your family and all the things you are doing that are building connected relationships in your home.

DEVELOPING COLLABORATIVE BEHAVIOURS

Listed below are some behaviours and habits that are present in families that seek to collaborate together. Read through them and check in with yourself and with your family to identify which ones you recognise and use.

You could use a traffic light system:

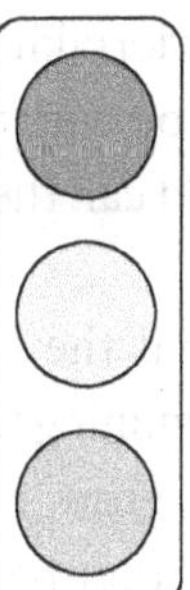

Circle in red the ones that are new to you

Circle in orange the ones that you recognise but don't feel confident in

Circle in green the ones that you recognise and use well

- Working towards a shared goal
- Being adaptable
- Involving everyone it is relevant to
- Purposefully seek feedback
- Being an active listener
- Able to be honest

- Able to share ideas
- Being respectful
- Able to see different perspectives
- Aiming for a win:win

The heart of unschooling

You don't need much to be able to unschool and to unschool well. It's not really about what you are physically able to provide, the activities you pay for, the resources you have or the size of your home. It is an educational philosophy that focuses on nurturing your child's natural curiosity and creating a life in which that can flourish. At the heart of it all is how your child views themself as a competent human being and a competent learner, how they feel about themself and how they feel about the people closest to them. It boils down to emotional safety and trust.

The time, effort and energy you can afford to put in place to support your child/ren is the biggest consideration when thinking about unschooling. Whatever your child's age, they need you. This participation and support looks different at different stages; nonetheless, when considering this path, you should be aware that it is not the lazy option and that there is a significant undertaking on your part. If not on your part, then who is going to be with your child when you can't be (for example, if you work), and can they be a continuation of your educational approach?

The relationship you are building with your child is the single most impactful element on their learning. From the beginning to the end of your unschooling life, you need to build, heal, grow, repair and nurture those relationships. For a child to feel like they belong, they need to know that they belong just as they are. They must be sure that who they are is loved, welcome and honoured. They need to feel safe and trusted, and trust the person who is helping them navigate the world.

Getting to know your child and being in tune with them is central to the unschooling life. When your child has a person by their side who they know will always be on their team, keep them safe, listen to them and hear what they are saying, this changes their relationship with themself and how they interact with the world for the better. They need someone who will work with them and support them in the things they want to do, someone who is present, available and attentive to their needs, and who partners them unwaveringly through life.

From this solid point your child can confidently express themself, explore with unbounded curiosity the world around them, and follow wherever that thread of curiosity leads them. They can be free from the shackles that steer them away from their heart choices and require them to conform to a standardised programme. Being radically accepted may mean that their learning is inconspicuous. They may prefer more time exploring more things, on their own terms, with extended periods of rest or quieter and more contemplative processes. This is the beauty, and the challenge, of being able to confidently navigate life and learning on their own terms. No one can guarantee what it looks like, and no one can guarantee what is being learned and when. Our confidence is knowing that curiosity and lifelong learner capabilities are being nurtured and enabled. That our children can look at themselves with love and compassion, make time for their mental health needs, and find joy, peace and ease in the choices they make, free from judgement and shame or the need to conform and comply at the cost of supressing or ignoring their own self.

The reality is that you do need more than one thing to be able to unschool, but the one thing that is going to keep you in good stead and the one thing that you cannot do without is your *relationship with your child*. If you base every decision you make on how it affects your relationship with your child, you can't go far wrong.

Principles to live by

- See your child for who they are.
- Enjoy your time together.

- People are more important than things.
- Work together in partnership.

Chapter 11

Teens, Screens and Socialisation

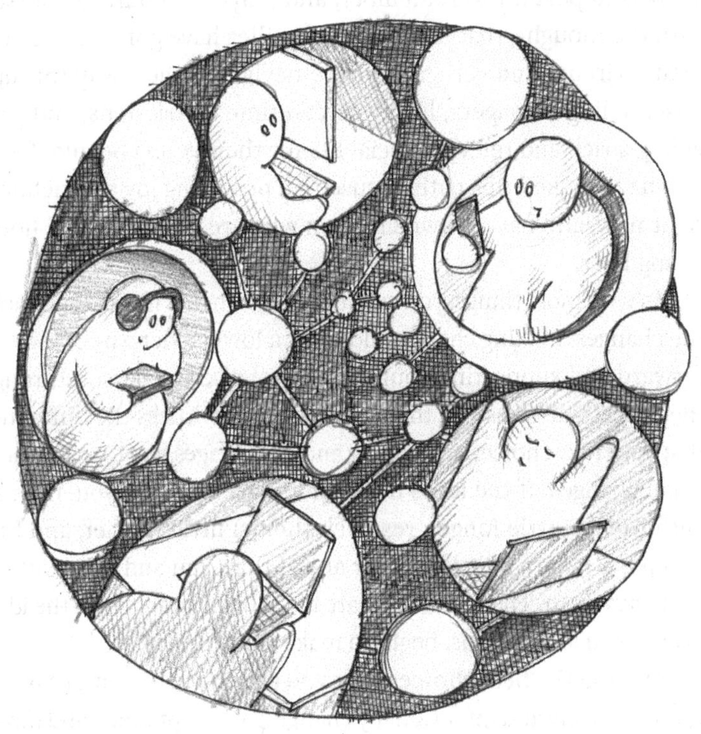

There are many questions that I am asked on a regular basis, things that race through the minds of many parents when they consider or begin unschooling. Here are the three most common:

What about teens? Is it too late to take them out of school and do something so different with them? How can they take their exams, or what happens if they don't want to take exams?

If I let my child choose what they did all day, they would spend all of it on a screen gaming/watching YouTube/posting on TikTok – surely that's not good for them?!

How will my child socialise if I take them out of school?

This chapter sets out to *begin* answering these questions from an unschooling perspective.

It is important to remember, and maybe encourage yourself with the thought, that many other families have gone before you. Many parents and caregivers have navigated their way through unschooling teenagers, lifting screen time restrictions, and providing a rich and relevant social life for their young people. Many folk have walked this path, focused on providing joy and richness right now, and have grown children who are living full and flourishing lives.

As with most things, you won't see the benefits if you don't make the changes. Making changes slowly is a low impact way of moving forward and supporting yourself and your young person through the process. It gives you the opportunity to witness the difference that your new choices are making and encourages you to make more small changes. If the ideas here don't make sense to you, then sit with them a little longer, research them a little further, and find families who are a little further ahead than you and observe/ask/chat with them. Then, when you are more comfortable with the idea, even if you are nervous, begin to make small changes.

Making the best choices that you can in each moment is one way of actively and intentionally changing your approach and direction. That's not to say that you will always make the right choice or that you won't retreat to the safety of old habits, but with grace and compassion you can press the reset button and simply try to do better next time. Taking one choice at a time creates big changes in the long run, without a sudden and abrupt overhaul, which can be disconcerting and disruptive.

The way to make better choices is to centre your child and put your relationship with them first. This might seem antithetical as a component to an educational approach, but if there is one thing to take away from this book it is it that your relationship with your child is key to unschooling. This idea is essentially what will inform the decisions you make, the changes you implement and the way you navigate life as a family.

Essentially you need to be happy in your own skin. While there can be periods of discombobulation through periods of change, they are easier to navigate if you know where you are going and why. They are easier to navigate if you are well informed and have support. They are easier to navigate when you make changes that suit your family and are rooted in relationship.

Removing teenagers from school

School is one way to learn, and it is being sold to us as the only way to learn. Our young people are put under tremendous strain at such a tumultuous time in their development. It is not surprising that with increasingly draconian measures being put in place in many secondary and high schools that our young people are struggling. They are responding the best way they know how to within the confines of what is possible. Once again, our child's behaviour is telling us something. Something is wrong and it is not your teen.

As young people enter adolescence, they undergo rapid changes in their cognitive, emotional and social development, making it an ideal time for unschooling to come into its own. It offers an environment that supports teenagers in exploring their passions and interests while fostering autonomy, critical thinking and personal growth. At a time in a young person's life when they are naturally thinking outside of the box, removing the confines of an immovable curriculum and facilitating their passions while giving them ownership over their choices works with the adolescent brain rather than resisting it. As an approach, unschooling enables young people to take ownership of their life and learning in relevant, engaging and meaningful ways. Real-world learning experiences foster curiosity, exploration and personal drive in concrete ways that are personally relevant to the young person's goals and aspirations.

Unschooling also provides a flexible and individualised approach to learning, allowing teenagers to learn at their own pace and accommodate their unique learning styles. This flexibility can be particularly beneficial for teenagers who may struggle in a traditional school setting due to learning differences, anxiety or social challenges. By creating a supportive environment tailored to your young person's individual needs, unschooling can help teenagers develop self-confidence, resilience and a strong sense of self-efficacy.

The difficulty is that no one can guarantee that your teen will take the pre-approved route into adulthood. They may not take 5–12 exams at the age of 16 or go to college. It might take them longer to find a part-time job or commit to any one thing. Without giving them a predetermined timeline it is highly likely that they will be confident going at their own pace and exploring all of their options.

Alice explained how she calms her fears when she starts to think about her teen daughter possibly taking exams (or not):

> “There is a question about qualifications and how do you get them to be employable if you're not doing a curriculum, if you're not following a specific pathway? I just keep working back from 'They'll find something they like, and they'll find something they want to do'. We can work out what they need to do to get there, and we can relax about the time frame a bit.

You have a beautiful opportunity to nurture strong and trusting relationships between your teenager and yourself. By actively supporting and guiding their learning journey, you can develop a deeper understanding of your teenager's interests, strengths and challenges. I mean, they are still teenagers who will enjoy swathes of time with their friends and cocoon themselves for hours on end, but the sense of connection that is present from the collaborative approach fosters open communication and mutual trust. This positively impacts your young person's emotional and social development, and provides them with an unwavering foundation from which they can explore the world.

Sally shared how things looked for her boys during their teenage years:

> "They became more specialised in the things they really enjoyed. I do think, as they've approached the teen years, that they do tend to see things a little bit more through the lens of, 'What will I do in the future?' Not always. They still will, 100 per cent, do something just for the fun of it. But there is that, 'Oh, I wonder maybe I should have a go at this', a little bit of that comes into it.
>
> As teens they rely on me less. I think that's definitely the case. They're even more autonomous, so they don't need me in the same way to facilitate. Sometimes I do still facilitate. I mean I'm looking out for events and groups and interesting things to bring to them. If I didn't do that, then I'm sure they would still be fine, they do so much more of that themselves. I guess I've always got my eye out on real life, as it were, for little connection points for them in the things they do.

Of course, the change in approach takes time to adopt. Many teenagers have been immersed in the school system for a long time and have absorbed the messages that tell of being a failure if you don't have good exam results, and have lost or buried their own internal drive. There will be a period of adjustment (see Chapters 3 and 4) and possibly a change in your family culture. Remember that this isn't school, so comparing what your young person is doing to their schooled peers is unhelpful. You now have a beautiful opportunity to help them rewrite their story and to consider all aspects of themself leading to better physical, mental and emotional wellbeing.

The following exercise will help you to get started.

STARTING POINT FOR TEENS

It can be difficult to not worry about taking certain exams at certain times. It is entirely possible for unschooled young people to take exams if and when they want to. It is also entirely possible to enter further education in other ways too, or not at all. There are many routes into adulthood and many ways to live a fulfilling life. In the same way we can become stuck in our thinking about what our teens should be doing (and when), so can they.

There are two questions you can discuss *with them* that may help to pick apart the routes possible before them.

First, what do they think they *should* be doing?

This will probably generate answers along the lines of subject studies and exams. This is the list that will most likely reveal what others have told them they need to be doing and the one we are moving away from.

Second, what would you *prefer* to be doing? What do you *want* to do?

This is tricker, and depending on your teen you may get anything from a long list of ideas to a shrug of the shoulders and an 'I don't know'. That's okay. It's a start, and both answers give you a clear indication of where your young person is at and what to do next.

Earlier in the book I talked about how unschooling is a partnership. When we are faced with young people who are burnt out or unsure about what they want to do, we can step in with offers and ideas. It is important to remain in tune with your teen and listen carefully to their opinions and responses, and don't give up. Take it slowly if you need to, be gentle with yourself and with your young person. There is no rush anymore – you can move at a speed that suits them now.

Beyond screen time

The ongoing discussions involving screens, screen use and screen time are an ever-present topic of conversation in unschooling circles. I am sure that we are all familiar with the mainstream rhetoric about the evils of screen time, but there is research that demonstrates the value of screen-based activities, usually gaming, that debunk and challenge widely held ideas about the effects of prolonged screen use.

Once upon a time fears over 'screen use' only meant TV, and for children and children's programmes this was limited to after-school hours and Saturday mornings. And still parents worried that their children's eyes would go square and their children would be better off doing something else. Everything new worried people once: the printing press, radio, novels, TV, computers, gaming, social media. New technology isn't the problem in and of itself; it is usually the fear that people hold on to and the challenge to their beliefs and ideas that it raises that become the stumbling block. Each new generation is faced with the tools and progress of the next generation.

Applying the principles of unschooling across all areas of your child's life will include considering limits and control over their screen use. It is true that the transition may be rocky. There may initially be increased use of technology, which may or may not subside after an initial period. What will probably happen, though, is that their attitude will change towards how they use this modern-day tool. With a shift in attitude around the use of screens, their use will become more purposeful and thoughtful.

Making changes slowly

One way to move from restricted to unrestricted technology use is to simply say 'yes' more often. 'Can I finish this game?' Yes. 'Can I have 10 more minutes?' Yes. 'Can I download this new app?' Yes. Changes can happen slowly and gently. If you have a child whose default is to pick up their tablet, and this has previously resulted in anxious comments or redirection from yourself, simply not commenting anymore could be a good place to start. This is an example of lower demands and creating ease in the situation, which works towards establishing that sense of safety in which your child can become confident that they won't be shamed for their choices or their devices removed or time-restricted.

Where it is a continued source of conflict and there are often discussions (or arguments) over its use, having an explicit conversation about making changes may be useful. These changes can still be made incrementally and with care. If you have older children or already have an open culture of discussion and collaboration, it might be worth talking about the new approach you are taking and being open with your child about the change of direction. This can include sharing feelings that may arise for you alongside giving them the opportunity to bring their thoughts and feelings to the discussion too.

Sorrel talked about their journey from restricted screen use to seeing the benefits of applying unschooling principles into this area too. Like most of us they were hesitant and came from a starting place of 'no/low screen use', but leant into their child's needs and prioritising their relationship with their son:

> " I was where a lot of us were at: I thought my kid would have no screens until at least three, and even then, there would still be no screens, and that we would play with pine cones in the woods.
>
> He just wanted to press the buttons on my phone. It had buttons at the time, in the dark ages. He just wanted to press the buttons on my phone, and it was unquenchable. It was impossible to redirect him. All the standard parenting suggestions were not working. We tried 20 minutes and we were just going to watch. There's this one video. It's a song, and it's called 'Pipkin', and it's beautiful, felted animation. And I would allow us to watch 'Pipkin', like, over and over again.
>
> Then my eldest turned three, and the meltdowns got bigger and bigger and bigger, and they became more and more and more violent. They'd always been violent, but he was small, and now he was getting bigger, and it was really hurting, and he started saying, 'I hate you'. And he was three, and I was like, there's something's gone wrong there. Horribly, horribly wrong. Watching videos was all he thought about, however much we restricted, it was all he thought about.
>
> So, because it was usually about screens that he would have these

big meltdowns, we started to gently ease up. We started lifting the lid and allowing it. He went into a total binge fest. It was really intense, and I wasn't allowed to move because he's PDA, so the proximity to me was really important. We sat together and would watch TV most of every day for years. As I was watching it with him, even despite myself, I started to notice the learning happening.

He started talking to me about what he was watching. He wasn't just numbing out. He's wanting to have these conversations about what we're watching. And that just developed. He started gaming, and we used to play *Moshi Monsters*, which was so good. The little characters have speech bubbles, and so I would have to read for him for hours a day. I'd just sit and read for him. Then one day I needed to go and stare at the ceiling for a bit and I went to lay down in another room. I heard him reading from the other room, and he'd never shown any interest in reading. I had no idea that he knew anything about it. I think he was four, so he was still quite little, and he was reading, and it appeared to have happened out of nowhere. That bolstered the feeling of being less fearful about what we were doing.

I've come in and out of anxiety about it, and I think there has been times where he's been really needing it. I just knew that this is what he needed, and I was going to try and provide whatever it was that he needed.

A big piece of the puzzle is being able to see it working right before you and understanding that your child isn't just being a consumer and that they're having conversations and that it's interactive. I look at my kids' screen time and how they engage with these amazing tools that we have.

He'll come in and out of it, but he does spend the majority of his time gaming. He's on a big server with loads of friends from an unschooling camp that I've collectively run. He's got these friends he knows in real life, and now they're all in *Minecraft* together, and it's like just an extension of the camp. And it's magical.

He will now very happily turn off his computer whenever that's necessary. If we need to go out, he does karate and aerial arts [acrobatics performed using ropes, silks or hoops that are suspended from the ceiling] and he'll happily turn it off.

It's important to note that as part of an unschooling family Sorrel is responding to their child, and they are involved as much in his gaming and watching as they are in facilitating karate and aerial. The relationship piece is what makes a significant difference to your child's interaction with technology and will also make a difference to how you view their interaction with it too.

Beyond the screen

Singling out screens as a resource and limiting their use creates its own problems. Treating screentime with the same consideration as physical art supplies, equipment for hobbies such as sailing or sewing, and not attaching feelings of shame to it releases your child to explore its potential and relevance in their life.

For yourself, it is helpful to begin to look beyond the screen, to move away from using the word 'screens'. It is better to begin to observe and take notice of what your child is using their PC/phone/tablet/console for. To see the art they are designing, the games they are playing, the content they are watching, the people they are communicating with, the music they are listening to, the languages they are learning, the podcasts they are subscribed to, the books they are listening to. Beyond the 'screen' is a whole world of learning and entertainment, meaning and joy.

BEYOND THE SCREEN

Suggestion One: Observe and witness

Take some time to observe and witness the things your child is using a technological device for. Observe and witness any strong feelings that arise while you are recording your observations.

- Are there activities you are happy that your young person is doing?
- Are there activities that you can see a little value in?
- Are there activities you feel are frivolous or time wasting?
- Are there activities you have an instant dislike towards?

At this point there is no need to do anything more than pause and notice any strong feelings you have.

Suggestion Two: Writing and journalling

Set aside some quiet time and find a comfortable spot for yourself. It does help if you are undisturbed, but just do the best you can.

- Write about those feelings you felt. Take a moment to reflect and write about those emotions. Try and name them, use descriptive language to describe how it felt, where you felt the feeling in your body and why you felt that way.
- Write about your experiences. Recall when that feeling arose, what activity you were observing and the thoughts you had.
- Reflect on your writing. Take a look at what you have written. Can you locate thoughts and reasons and identify patterns? Do you recognise scripts you have that are from your upbringing, schooling or social expectations? Can you recognise those feelings as yours and own them?
- Consider your own regulation. Take time to identify what helps you feel better. Write down some ideas that you can come back to when strong feelings arise for you.

Suggestion Three: Observe and witness

Return often to observing and witnessing what your child is doing. Observe the activities they are doing, engage in the things they are doing, recognise the learning and lean into the joy they are experiencing.

Suggestion Four: Writing and journalling

Return to writing and journalling your thoughts. Remember that the feelings you have are yours and writing them down can be a useful way to process them as well as give you one way to regulate yourself. Having things written down can help you to consider what words to use when you need to talk through your thoughts and feelings with others too.

Chloe told me about how she learned to crochet. It involved several different internet sites, search engines and social media platforms as well as a good understanding of herself:

> I saw a bunch of images on Pinterest, a bunch of my friends crocheting, and I thought, I want to do that. So I watched this YouTube tutorial. I got so confused because they were doing it too slow on the video. I found out that if I go on to a normal video where it's for pros to do and I turn the sound off and just watch what they did with the hand moves to myself, then I can do it. And then every time I didn't know what a stitch looked like, I would Google it, and try and get my stitch to look like that and go, 'Right? So that's a double crochet'. I've learned terms. I did that in literally two weeks because I just sat down and went, I want to make a bat. And then I made a bat, and I just forced myself to figure it out on the way. And I learned Amro Gumi, I learned how to do that literally just starting on a difficult project and pushing through. If I get stuck on a bit, I'll just Google it quickly, turn the YouTube video sound off, because when people talk, I get confused.

Becoming comfortable with screen time

Shared experiences contribute to the strong relationships we are cultivating and are essential to unschooling. They contribute to your child's sense of self, including how they view the things they are passionate about. Joining our children in what they are doing, or, in the very real case that their skill and enthusiasm in gaming or the use of different technologies exceeds your own, supporting them in that pursuit in other ways is one way to engage with them.

Watching films together, playing computer games together, communicating via family group chats and sending gifs or links via private message, learning viral dances together, asking your child how to craft an item in *Minecraft* or figuring out together why the Wi-Fi connection has slowed down and how to reset it – there are lots of ways to facilitate what your child is doing:

- Observe what it is they are doing and what the interest is, and then explore websites, research related games and related activities, games, groups and conferences that are linked.

- Watch, rather than play. Sit with them in the same room. Give them as much attention as they need or simply be alongside them as they play, maybe doing your own thing.
- Ask them about it – their score – or new mods – or what the new levels are like. Be interested.
- Be generous with your time, space and resources. Make sure they have the right equipment and that it works well.
- Say 'yes' as much as you can and feel comfortable with doing at this point, and then say 'yes' a little more.

Rebecca shared how coming together as a family over technology use has built and strengthened their family dynamics:

> "Technology has been crucial to the children, because we have been at home. It's one of the few ways that my daughter has been able to connect with people while her brother recovers. And it's been brilliant because it's still emotional connection, isn't it? People think, 'Oh, that's not real'. Or others say, 'Well, we've got a friend over, so you don't need to use the computer now'. It's never a connecting thing, whereas for us, now, it's a hugely connecting thing, whether it's between us or between them and their friends.

Throughout this book, myself and those who have contributed have spoken at ease about their children's use and love of technology in their life and learning. It is as natural and readily available and used as books, art materials and bike riding. Removing the stigma around screen use **opens up possibilities** for those who wish to explore it, and with us alongside them to share, celebrate and guide them enables us all to navigate new things with curiosity together.

Socialisation and belonging

It's the number one question that new home educators ask, 'How will my child learn to socialise if they are home educated?'

We are largely under the misconception that children want and need to be with large groups of other children for most of the time to develop social skills. It is a ridiculous notion that children will learn how to interact with each other by being with their peers who are equally as socially immature and unaware as they are. There is more to socialising than playing with your friends, and living in the real world provides plenty of opportunity to interact with others in a variety of ways. You do not, however, get provided with an automatic social group, complete with 30 members, all situated in a small geographical location, when you are home educating (see Table 11.1).

Table 11.1. Socialisation in the real world

School vs. unschool	
School groups are automatic groupings	You will need to find your local home ed families
Schooled children largely spend all day with the same 30 children	You can choose who you meet up with and for how long
Schooled children have very little time for genuine social interaction	Unschooled children can (if they want to) spend many hours using and developing social skills with others
Schooled children are predominantly in same-aged groups	Unschooled children can have friends across mixed age groups and witness, use and develop skills with those across multi generations and in real-life scenarios, e.g. going to the library, using public transport, shopping at the market

For others the worry is that their child is unwilling and unable to leave the house, and the question of socialising lies heavily on them. Or rather, the expectation of others. When we look at this through the lens of unschooling – accepting what is and nurturing the unique child we have – it can mean that interacting with large groups and meeting with other children might not be right for your child right now.

Nicola described how small their family's world became when her children left school and how she leaned into what was needed. This led, in turn, to deep and meaningful friendships for both her children:

> When my son came out of school, we retreated from the world. We had some home-educated friends from when he'd home educated the first time. There were a few regular events. There was a forest school, it was once a week, and I think that probably started up pretty much straight away and he would do that.
>
> My daughter has got three best friends who have all been home educated, but she didn't go to groups with them. She couldn't handle groups apart from forest school. I guess forest school is the big thing she did. She did forest school for maybe 18 months. We basically couldn't go to other groups.
>
> My daughter was probably more adaptable at that age than my son, but she soon became unadaptable. She's been so lucky because she is, at heart, quite introverted, and she needed a few years of not having to socialise a lot and being okay on her own, because she's now confident and comfortable, and I think she needed all that time to just be herself.

The schooled concept of socialising is really wonky. Forced association is not the same as socialising. Only being able to talk to your peers in controlled ways, such as completing a task in a lesson or at controlled times (e.g. in the playground) is not an ideal way to make friends or learn how to interact with others.

Unschooling, on the other hand, enables young people to form strong core relationships with key people, and creates a blueprint for trustworthy and loving relationships in the future. Being immersed in real-life interactions in a variety of contexts provides experience of meaningful interactions. Being part of a community of people where your contribution is valued and nurtured **cultivates a sense of belonging** and genuine connection.

We want to make life better, enjoyable and interesting in the ways that your child finds better, enjoyable and interesting. Sometimes this means making home peaceful and cosy and fostering their primary relationships. At other times it may mean seeking out social opportunities for them. As May Ling explained:

> We could see that they wanted to see their friends more often. So,

> their friends come to our house and hang out for the day. We're lucky because we have a garden, and they're doing role-play, complex or social play, navigating conflict and stuff, although not always successfully.

Socialising comes in all different shapes and forms – chatting over the fence with a neighbour, asking the librarian about certain books at the library, playing with peers, sending a parcel at the post office, playing online, working on a project together at an interest group. Children often relate to their peers (but not always), but being part of a community and feeling a sense of worth and belonging in the group they are in, no matter how small or big, is what cultivates confidence in interacting with other people.

The home-educating world is full to the brim with social opportunities. There are groups popping up all over the place. In all honesty the real challenge is learning what to say 'no' to and finding the right groups for your child – being responsive to their needs, trusting in the process, being comfortable with your child's preferred level of social interaction, providing the right opportunities without being invested in the outcome and being by their side and supporting them when they are interacting with others.

Rebecca shared how playing online with friends has been crucial to her son developing social skills as it provides an alternative and safe context in which to develop his social interactions when in-person connections have been difficult for him:

> “My son plays *Minecraft*, and he plays with random people we don't know but we're there and we see the benefits of it. We've seen how he can use those environments to say things that he doesn't feel able to with in-person interactions. When I play with him with another one of his friends, if his friend does something to me in game, he'll get protective, in a way that would feel too emotionally vulnerable in real life. I've seen lots of amazing things in that space like having just one-to-one partnerships for him to be able to sort out conflict in that scenario online. He will play online, and then he will video call with someone, and they work out so much together.

Taking your time

Big unschooling questions can seem overwhelming. When it becomes a thought so big that it stops you from changing anything, it is also good to sit with that thought a while and examine it. Doing your research and understanding what something involves so that you can get a good idea of what you are doing is a sensible approach. Whatever it is that occupies your mind, remember that you don't need to change everything at once. Take your time. Start with the things that do make sense, make changes, however small, one choice at a time. **Lead with curiosity** rather than be held back by fear, and step into a journey of discovery, taking one step at a time and trying one thing at a time.

In the same way, we can open up our child's world by removing the barriers they are facing: relieving the pressure of exams if your teen needs to recover from poor school experiences and find a different way forward; embracing the world that technology has to offer and doing it with abandon; finding community where your child is welcome just as they are and can make connections on their own terms. Removing these constraints, and others, releases your child into the same journey of discovery.

Over time you will look back and realise how different your lives are now compared to before. I don't want to give the impression that it is all unicorns and rainbows, because it is still life! There will be situations that are difficult that you may need to navigate as a family, but removing the things you can makes a big difference. You will see this growing, peaceful, joyful life full of learning that has been cultivated by and rooted in respectful relationships.

Principles to live by

- Make the best choices that you can in each moment.
- Open up possibilities.
- Cultivate a sense of belonging.
- Lead with curiosity.

Chapter 12

Unleashing a Life of Learning

The easiest way to describe unschooling is that it is not school. You can take most aspects of school and schooling and remove them from your home education set-up and you will have begun unschooling. In fact, an unschooling family recognises that the hidden curriculum of school, as much as the practical elements, are mostly detrimental to the flow, joy and ease of unschooling on a daily basis. The foundations and aims of school are entirely different to those of unschooling. This is why in Chapter 1 we walked through what your goals are and why the principles and ideas that unschooling is built on are important to figure out. Without them to steer your decision making you can get caught up in schoolish thinking and ways.

Unschooling is not about what your child is doing and learning. This is why there cannot be an unschooling curriculum. Unschooling is interested in the reasons behind the activity. How did this child make this decision? How did they choose this question? Why are they playing with that toy? What do they find fascinating in this activity? What is drawing them in and holding their attention? What makes them feel comfortable enough to be in this place playing this game? This is how we end up unable to answer the question, 'What does a typical day look like?' with uniformity. It's not about the tangible nature of what unschoolers are doing; it's about the culture they live in and the principles that guide the choices that brought them to where they are now and the things they are doing today.

By the time most unschoolers reach adulthood they can be doing a great many things that schooled adults are doing. You could take two adults in the same job and on the surface not know which one went to school and which one was unschooled. The difference at this point is how they got there and the reasons they are in that field of work. The difference is in their life experiences, how they view themselves, how they view others and their understanding of their place in the world.

Unschooling really asks you to consider not only what your life can be like without school, but what it can be like if school had never existed in your life, in your community and in your culture.

Sarah has four unschooled children. They have been living as an unschooling family for over a decade and she is a strong advocate, speaker and unschooling mentor for other unschooling families. Like many parents her observations of her children and listening and responding to them is the daily practice that has led to years of building trust, respect and insight into what children are capable of when they don't have school in the mix. I asked her how she came to discover unschooling:

> " Like many families who find themselves out of school, there was an event that was the final straw, if you like, but I was always, I was always very, very warm to it since noticing how little my kids really needed instruction from, like, birth, so I was open to it. By the time we decided to really pull the kids out of school properly we'd already had a year out of school with my oldest, and the only reason that they'd gone back into school then was because she asked to go back. And I think that was partly in response to the fact that we had a fourth child in that year. So that was quite a big, lots of things were happening. My mother-in-law had died and we renovated a house. There's lots of things and I think she probably just wasn't quite sure where she was and probably needed a bit more than what she was maybe getting, and her go-to at that point, even at seven years old, was school. I was like, 'Okay, well, sure you can go back to school if you want'. We were, we were already quite connected in a home-schooling community in South Australia where we're from, so we had this toe in the whole time. I had these wonderful cheerleading friends who kept saying, 'When are you going to pull the kids out properly?' 'Why are you still doing school?' 'Come on this trip with us.' 'Come on this camp.' I really had a heart for it from very early on. To be honest, by the time it got to that final straw, I was already up to my waist in the water. So that was it.
>
> It wasn't really a very big deal by that point. I did have this one child who was probably your typical 'school refuser', as other people like to call them. They're kids that know their own mind. It was very obvious they literally didn't know what to do with this kid. They didn't have the tools or the resources, they had no idea what to do with a child like mine. School just did not make any sense anymore at that point. We could have continued flogging a dead horse, which was ridiculously painful and insulting to him because he knew he wasn't supposed to be there already, or we could just get on with living because by the time you're at that point, school was a massive inconvenience. It's a

really big pain in the arse. I have to get these kids up out of bed who don't want to get out of bed. I have to stop them from playing. They just want to play. I have to make them go to this place where everyone tells them what to do all the time. They don't want to do that and none of it really made sense.

Leaving school behind

Imagine a world in which school doesn't exist and never has done. What expectations about children and learning might be different or not even enter your mind if you weren't familiar with a schooled education? Could it be possible that children would be found playing for years longer than they do, because no one has required them to sit at a desk instead? Could it be that children would spend more time doing the things that interested them and that they felt competent in because no one has told them that they should be learning something else or that they need to improve in other areas? How would you live your life and how would your child live theirs?

Your child won't be shamed for getting things wrong, they won't be required to be up and ready by 9am, they won't have to sit any longer than they can do, they won't need to ask permission to go to the toilet, they can play with the people they choose, they can eat when they're hungry, move when their body needs to, and not be separated from their family until they are ready to in their own time.

I wonder what living and learning would look like in your family if you removed teachers, timetables, curriculums, subjects, projects, tests and a great many other expectations that have been passed to us via our schooling?

Living an unschooling life is really just living a life, as Sarah put it during her interview:

> “What I want people to really kind of tap into is that this is not an experiment. This is how humans have lived for the majority of human existence. We're not doing something crazy that's untested at all. What we're really doing is just peeling back all the stuff that's been layered on top of human life for the last particularly 200–300 years. And we're

> getting back to what it means to be a human. And therefore, it's completely natural to trust our kids even when things are hard, right? Like, you're going through something hard, or your kids are going through something hard, and you're like, 'Oh, it's actually going to be okay even though this is hard on us, it's actually going to be okay'. And obviously that can look different all the time, can't it? When we're actually living, how we're meant to be living in full trust of our kind, that's essentially it. That's your job. That's it. That's all you have to do. You don't have to teach anyone to read. You don't have to worry about what they're eating. Don't have to worry about making them go to bed. You don't have to make them brush their teeth. You're like, 'I gotta hold my kid's hand right now, I can do that for hours'. That's it.

School is a strange notion and a relatively new one in the history of the world. Living together in families and communities and growing and learning alongside trusted adults in loving, nurturing and accepting cultures has been the way humans have grown into adulthood for thousands of years. Of course there are differences – our young people now have more options, more opportunities, more choices, more possibilities. Life has more to offer when they are ready, willing and able to explore those options for themselves, with you alongside them, unleashing a life of learning. Or, as most unschoolers come to see it, simply living their life.

Can you imagine a life without school? What would this mean for your child? What would it mean if today your child didn't go to school? What would your child do instead? What would your child choose to do? Would they be equipped or know how to make a choice that was in alignment with their core being? Would they feel confident in making choices that filled their lives with abundance, delight, **peace and ease**? Here are some of the things that go on regularly in our house:

- Play computer games (I know that's top of a lot of children's lists)
- Play with friends
- Walk the dog

- Read a book
- Play with face paints
- Build with LEGO
- Sit in a den
- Climb a tree
- Make slime
- Craft and make models with paper
- Paint mini figures
- Digital art work
- Write creative stories.

It's beginning to look like one of those lists that circulate for 'things to do in the school holidays', and honestly, it can be a bit like that. When school is taken out of the equation, a whole new world of possibilities presents itself. My children have never been to school, and I have often found myself wondering how others have the time for it.

While the majority of families are spending their time together trying to get up and out to school in the morning, and filling their evenings with clubs and homework, we are enjoying being together, and the children are enjoying the things they are doing. No one is setting an immovable timetable or daily schedule. In fact, we rarely talk about learning directly at all. I never ask my children, 'What would you like to learn?' or 'What project would you like to work on?' We almost never do something because our conscious aim is to learn about it. Of course, there is nuance here. Sometimes you will hear phrases in our house like, 'I never knew that before!' or 'I'm going to look that up and find out' or 'This exhibition looks interesting, can we go?' – which are all indicators of learning happening and plans forming.

Turning education upside down

Unschooling is the very opposite of school. I can't think of one aspect of mainstream schooling that contributes to an unschooling learning approach. No one here will tell you what to learn, or when to learn it. No one here will ask you to set your learning intention before you begin to play a game, and no one will test you or ask you to show your learning on a worksheet or diary entry when you are done. No one here will tell you that you must study literacy every day, or that you only have an hour this week to work on the art project you are doing. No one here is going to test you on your times tables and grade you in front of your peers. Yet again, there is nuance here too. My children might laugh and play with numbers while they are spending money and gathering tickets at the arcade. One of mine loves a journal and regularly writes her thoughts in it. It's not that these things don't happen; it's that they *can* happen, and when they do, they have no reference to doing it because school says it is necessary.

Living a life without school requires us to leave every idea or emotion or reason that is attached to a schooled idea behind you. This is why taking the time to adjust is essential. Unschooling needs your children and you to address your experiences and struggles with school and purposefully heal from them so that you can build something new. School is often part of your journey towards unschooling, how you got here and your initial reasons for taking a new approach, but for unschooling to flourish, at some point your school experiences and attachment to schooled ideas need to be left behind.

Living a life, one choice at a time

When we leave school behind us, in thought and in practicality, and we view the life before us and all its possibilities with **curiosity and wonder**, we can also see that the world is big and wide. The options before us are vast and the opportunities innumerable. Granted, this can be an overwhelming concept, but it is also an exciting truth. When we recognise that everything is connected, we can afford ourselves the time to focus on the things we love, the things that fascinate us, the ideas that light us up, the spaces that captivate our imaginations, knowing that it will equip us for whatever lies ahead in the future.

Learning with abandon by actively responding to our natural curiosity and nurturing our innate drive to discover more about the world is an individualised path crafted in the comfort of your family. An unschooling life happens one choice at a time. Those choices are made utilising what you know about life and learning. They are built on the tenets of relational ideals such as trust, acceptance, respect and kindness.

Life becomes less about whether or not you are unschooling and more about whether you are consciously and intentionally living a joyful and peaceful life, where your child can explore their interests in a loving, supportive and vibrant environment. It can be fancy and exciting. And when we consider the endless possibilities, it feels like the world is your oyster. For some families it can be the springboard for an adventurous life full of travel, or rethinking your own choices and instigating a change of direction in career, or unearthing your heart's desire and relocating your family. For most it is simply making the best choice that you can in this moment: supporting your child's interest in gaming; placing ingredients for slime making on a repeat order; making pancakes for breakfast together; watching the same film for the 364th day in a row. Things that become everyday occurrences peppered with postcards from relatives on holiday, sitting up to celebrate the Summer Solstice, trying out a new event locally, introducing a new slime recipe or going to a gaming convention (preferably on a week day).

We get to do the exciting and novel things we want to, when we want to, and that includes not doing them if we don't want to (one informed choice at a time, remember). We have the opportunity to engage with the big wide world, but equally we have the opportunity to slow right down. To take things at our own pace and make conscious and intentional decisions based on our ability, wants and needs in this moment. To thoughtfully consider what it is that we want right now and what we are able to do.

Having the world open, big and wide before us does give us the opportunity to embrace an abundance of joy and endless possibilities, but it also affords the opportunity to find joy in more simple things. It allows us not only to scream 'yes!' to the big sensational things, but to also find inspiration and peace in our day-to-day. It affords us the ability to be able to say 'No, that's not for me right now, I am content and at peace with collecting stones/sitting on the beach/watching cartoons/playing board games/meeting my friends at the park'.

It isn't about what you are doing or how exciting your life appears to be to others. It is about how you make the decisions that lead you to live this life you are living. Slowing down and thoughtfully considering your choices and your responses during your day-to-day living.

As Sarah put it when I interviewed her,

> One of my kids can't ride a bike. He doesn't want to, he hasn't tried, he's not interested. I don't know if he will one day. He likes walking. He's not interested in riding a bike. He's 14 tomorrow. Not bothered about riding a bike. No one cares. His friends don't care. It's not a thing. But I'm aware that other people probably think that's super-weird. He also he doesn't want to wear shoes, ever, where he has to tie laces.

The art of observation

As unschooling parents, we get comfortable with the ongoing questions and shedding deeply entrenched schooled ideas because it becomes part of our process of purposefully living. These questions and concerns that crop up don't become an all-consuming worry, but we can approach them with the same curiosity and wonder we do with other thoughts that we have. We can stop worrying about all the things that our children are not doing (because when we see the big wide world we notice that there are a lot of things they are not doing) and enjoy and celebrate the things they are doing.

Sarah shared her perspective on being comfortable with an unschooling life:

> They've all got these things. They've all got these things that they're amazing at, so who gives a shit if they can't read until they're 12 or tie their laces or sleep in their own bed or whatever? To me that's

another distinction of this lifestyle. You've got time to, like, notice that stuff. And maybe because we're not so worried, and we're not so busy pushing kids through this schooled process, we've got time to notice the other things that they do that are wanting to live a good life and relating with other humans.

Shifting your life perspective from a schooled lens to an unschooled one takes a shift in your thinking, as I am sure you know by now. This last exercise asks you to home in on the aspects you are currently finding challenging and reframe them through the lens of unschooling. So much of how we approach a situation, and the choices we make, depends on how we feel about and look at the world.

REFRAMING YOUR THOUGHTS

This is simply an exercise in observation – observing yourself, your thoughts and your feelings. No solutions. No answers. No steps forward. Simply practise the art of observation and knowing yourself.

Write down a situation you are currently finding difficult in relation to your child's choices, learning or the way they are showing up in life.

> For example: Whenever we are at home Greg spends all his time gaming. He doesn't want to do anything else no matter how many different things I offer him. The house is full of ideas and options, but he doesn't want to do them. It is difficult to get him to stop when we need to go out or when he needs to eat or sleep. He doesn't talk about anything else other than his game and isn't interested in doing anything with me.

Form these thoughts into a single statement:

> For example: I am finding the amount of time Greg spends gaming difficult.

Take this statement and consider two perspectives:

It's hard because:	It's easy because:
I don't understand the game or what is so compelling about it. I can't play with him because I don't have the skills, he is more advanced than me and it is frustrating for everyone. I don't like that it occupies all of his time, and he is single-minded about it. There seems to be very little educational value in it, and it causes friction between us	He is enjoying himself and it is lovely to see him immersed in something that he finds compelling. I do love listening to him enthusiastically recount what he has done (even if I don't understand it all), and I can see how he is building online friendships. It's easy for me to facilitate by investing in the right equipment, and I can see how well regulated he is and how he is able to concentrate for long periods of time

The more we can lean into the ease, joy and positives, the more ease, joy and positives will be experienced.

Learning to be

At some point down the line, you will look back and realise that you haven't even thought about what your child is learning today, and you will be getting on with the business of living a life. When we truly understand in our core that learning happens all the time, we can truly consider what it is we want to be doing and how we want to spend our time without worrying about whether our child is learning anything or what they are learning.

Unleashing a life of learning really requires us to stop focusing on our child's education and future and start focusing on our life and the conscious choices we make now, today, in this moment. Life isn't about meeting the targets and expectations of others, marching to someone else's timeline.

Make conscious choices about how you spend your time and afford the same thing to your children. How they will know what they want to do in the future will be by deciding what they want to do now. How they know what will light them up and what they are good at in adulthood will be easier to discover when they are given a life now that enables them to do the things they enjoy and that they are good at now. Living in a family culture where they are accepted fully as they are, where their choices and interests are valued, building their knowledge and understanding and belief in themselves is what will equip them for their life, both now and in the future.

Children get good at making choices by actively making choices. Young adults trust themselves by being trusted as young people. They know how to manage and process feelings as adults having had someone who co-regulated with them and sat with them through those same feelings as a young person. They know how to critically think about ideas and proposals by having their questions and criticisms listened to and taken seriously.

The best way to prepare children for their future is not with early intervention or early instruction but to give them what they need right now, to explore the world in ways that are meaningful to them, and to do so with a trusted and supportive partner alongside them.

All these moments, the endless cake baking, the spillages, the sibling fights, the (hundreds of) hours of *Minecraft*, the travelling to museums, galleries, classes and events, activities that take over the house, unopened subscription boxes, meeting your favourite YouTuber day out, navigating time zones for online gatherings, days sat on an empty beach with friends, evenings spent BBQing sausages long past when most other families have headed home, nights spent watching the planets, early mornings just to see the sunrise, impromptu swimming in the local lake when you have no spare clothes with you, getting lost in mazes, exploring castles, snuggling on the sofa together, singing loudly in the car to their favourite songs, bedtime stories until they are well into their teen years, searching for butterflies/birds/mushrooms/trees with local experts. All of that, and most importantly, how you respond to them, support them and love them through it all, these are the moments that connect together to make a day, a month, a year, a lifetime.

Sarah shared her take on this:

> “You can have so much fun. If you lean into stuff that you never ever imagined you'd be okay with, which I know sounds scary to people, because they're not okay with even thinking about those things. That has been the most magical thing for me. All the things that when my kids were small and that I thought I should be worried about, and my kids have pushed the limits on most of that stuff, and I'm not worried about anything at all.
>
> We're literally watching them become adults before our eyes. When you've been an unschooling family, and you haven't been forcing curriculum on them, you've really just been trusting that it's all going to be fine. And then, in front of your eyes, it's all fine. It's like oh, this is really cool.
>
> I am constantly surprised like every day, even though relatively seasoned at this, I'm still every day amazed at the stuff that they do and say and think and come up with, and literally all I do is like feed them and, like, give them my credit card.

Leaving school behind in every possible way is years of ongoing work. Approaching with curiosity every fear that arises, every doubt, every time we feel a knot in our chest about what our child is doing, every time we compare them to their friend or a schooled neighbour, every time their choice challenges us or we do not share their opinion. Being comfortable with being uncomfortable and being able to sit and observe and question ourselves: What is this thought? Where did it originate? Is it true?

It is undeniably challenging to question everything that you once held to be true. It is an enormous task to reconsider and rebuild ideas about childhood, learning, relationships and life. Unschooling nurtures a growth mindset, the idea that we are always learning, not limited to facts and figures supplied by others, but it relies on our own sense of curiosity, undertaking our own research, and engaging with our own sense of awe and wonder across all aspects of life. It is built on the very notion that there is always more to know and always more to discover, which, in turn, means that our ideas about things will change, develop and grow over time. For parents, being at ease with unschooling comes when you are at ease with this process.

Final thoughts

Unschooling is living a full and complete life as if school didn't and never has existed. Once you have tamed a great many fears and worries (and become comfortable with the process of doing so when they arise again) and turn your gaze onto all the amazing things that your child can and does do, unschooling can really begin to come into its own. It's fascinating to watch your child learn to swim without lessons (when they are ready). It is inspiring the hours that they can concentrate on things they are passionate about. It's incredible the quantity of facts and figures they can recall on their favourite topic. And mind-boggling how little of the stuff you previously thought was needed to parent and educate your child is useful.

Unschooling is an educational philosophy built on two core principles: children are able to learn, and learn well, when their natural curiosity is cultivated. They are fully capable of knowing what piques their interest. They are fully capable of knowing when they need a challenge or when they need to repeat the same activity again. They know whether they need to read about an idea first or watch someone or just jump straight in and do it. They know. It is your role to honour and nurture that knowing.

Which leads nicely to the second core principle, because, as with all things, they are inseparable and intricately connected. For optimal learning to happen children need to live in families and communities where they are nurtured and accepted just as they are. This builds a strong sense of self. When you partner them in their exploration of the world, get to know them and respond to them in ways that are suited to them, they can unashamedly carry this into their future lives and learning.

The symbiotic nature between these two core principles cultivates a life where your child can flourish and thrive in whatever direction that takes them.

I am sharing a final thought provided by Sarah. I have chosen it because it demonstrates the fusion between these two core ideas in such a simple and beautiful example:

> “I just want to give other parents the confidence that kids know pretty much everything they need to know. And yes, we're here to guide and facilitate and help them, but they just don't need half what other people think they do know. That's really evident from birth, like the stuff that they just know how to do by being with us. They do need us, they do need to be with people who already know how to do stuff. And then they just watch us. My son and I were walking yesterday by the canal and there's a swan family and there were mum, dad, seven babies, and they were in the canal in the water. The babies were just copying the parents. I would say they were they were old enough to swim but they were only probably, like, days old. I would say they're quite small. They were all curving their necks in the water and then back out again and the parents were on the outside just watching them and the babies were just doing what the parents were doing. Then today I saw them and the babies were asleep on the path alongside the canal, all seven babies and the mum and dad were just standing there while the babies slept. And I'm like, far out. That's so simple.

Unschooling is an educational philosophy that goes beyond the tick-box exercise of ‘What is my child learning?’ It permeates through our lives. The goal is not to be educated as such but to cultivate a life of learning. Just as you can't separate play and learning, you can't separate life and learning, not once you are fully unschooling. Learning happens as easy and naturally as breathing. No coercion, no external motivation. It is seamlessly connected to who you are and how you live your life. Unschooling is an invitation to live fully, purposefully and intentionally, taking what can seem to be an unusual and extraordinary way to live (to others) and making it second nature in your home.

Principles to live by

- Cultivate a life of peace and ease.
- Approach life with curiosity and wonder.
- Unleash a life of learning.

Recommended Further Reading

Blake, Boles (2014) *The Art of Self Directed Learning: 23 Tips for Giving Yourself an Unconventional Education*. Tells Peak Press.

Blakemore, Sarah-Jayne (2019) *Inventing Ourselves: The Secret Life of the Teenage Brain*. Black Swan.

Chen, Iris (2021) *Untigering: Peaceful Parenting for the Deconstructing Tiger Parent*. Untigering Press.

Deci, Edward L. (1996) *Why We DO What We Do: Understanding Self-Motivation*. Penguin Books.

Faber, Adele and Mazlish, Elaine (2022) *How to Talk so Kids Will Listen and Listen so Kids Will Talk*. Lagom.

Fisher, Naomi (2021) *Changing Our Minds: How Children Can Take Control of Their Own Learning*. Robinson.

Fricker, Eliza (2023) *Can't Not Won't: A Story About a Child Who Couldn't Go to School*. Jessica Kingsley Publishers.

Gatto, John Taylor (2017) *Dumbing Us Down: The Hidden Curriculum of Compulsory Schooling*. 25th Anniversary Edition. New Society Publishers.

Gopnik, Alison (2017) *The Gardner and the Carpenter: What the New Science of Child Development Tells Us about the Relationship Between Parents and Children*. Vintage.

Gray, Peter (2015) *Free to Learn: Why Unleashing the Instinct to Play Will Make Our Children Happier, More Self-Reliant, and Better Students for Life*. Basic Books.

Gray, Peter and Riley, Gina (2015) 'Grown unschoolers' evaluations of their unschooling experiences: Report I on a survey of 75 unschooled adults.' *Other Education: The Journal of Educational Alternatives* 4, 2, 8–32.

Greene, Ross W. (2021) *The Explosive Child: A New Approach for Understanding and Parenting Easily Frustrated, Chronically Inflexible Children*. Sixth Edition. Harper Paperbacks.

Holt, John (1989) *Learning All the Time: How Small Children Begin to Read, Write, Count, and Investigate the World, Without Being Taught*. Da Capo Books.

Holt, John (1995) *How Children Fail*. Da Capo Press.

Holt, John (2017) *How Children Learn*. 50th Anniversary Edition. Da Capo Lifelong Books.

Kohn, Alfie (1999) *Punished by Rewards: The Trouble with Gold Stars, Incentive Plans, A's, Praise, and Other Bribes*. Houghton Mifflin Co.

Kohn, Alfie (2006) *Unconditional Parenting: Moving from Rewards and Punishments to Love and Reason*. Atria Books.

Laricchia, Pam (2012) *Free to Learn: Five Ideas for a Joyful Unschooling Life*. Living Joyfully Enterprises.

Liberti, Lainie (2022) *Seen, Heard & Understood: Parenting & Partnering with Teens for Greater Mental Health*. [Independently published.]

Llewellyn, Grace (1997) *The Teenage Liberation Handbook: How to Quit School and Get a Real Life and Education*. Thorsons.

Mitra, Sugata (2019) *The School in the Cloud: The Emerging Future of Learning*. Corwin.

Mountney, Ross (2008) *Learning Without School: Home Education*. Jessica Kingsley Publishers.

Pattison, Harriet (2016) *Rethinking Learning to Read*. Educational Heretics Press.

Pink, Daniel H. (2008) *Drive: The Surprising Truth About What Motivates Us*. Canongate Books.

Richards, Akilah S. (2020) *Raising Free People: Unschooling as Liberation and Healing Work*. PM Press.

Rosen, Michael (2015) *Good Ideas: How to Be Your Child's (and Your Own) Best Teacher*. John Murray.

Ryan, Richard M. and Deci, Edward L. (2017) *Self-Determination Theory: Basic Psychological Needs in Motivation, Development, and Wellness*. Guilford Press.

Thomas, Alan and Pattison, Harriet (2008) *How Children Learn at Home*. Continuum.